D0020867

PB— CRL—140

The
PhotoReading
Whole Mind System

I thought I would give you feedback on my success in PhotoReading since using the book.

I wanted to get my master's degree. I tried taking a course 18 months ago. I was not able to complete it, because it took so much time and my grades were not good (C or D before I dropped the course).

I tried the PhotoReading method on some Navy correspondence courses, and it seemed to work well. I needed to test it for real, though. In the fall of 1993, I enrolled in two courses at the local junior college in business law and marketing. I used only the PhotoReading whole mind system.

The results were astounding. With no more effort than just going to class, I received not just A's, but I got the highest grade on every test in both classes. The best part was that I still had plenty of time with my family.

People at work and my family all say that what I am doing is impossible. I would have agreed with them one year ago, but instead I show them the transcripts to prove my progress. And still they do not believe.

I certainly am impressed.

Randy Now

I got a promotion at work.

I am now the computer administrator for my company. I am in charge of the computer network including all maintenance, trouble shooting, documentation, and purchasing.

This happened after only 45 days at the new job, and I have to say in all honesty that it would not have happened if not for PhotoReading. Every time there was a computer problem at work, I would go home that night and dedicate 1/2 hour or so to PhotoReading books on the subject. When I went back to work the next day, I usually had a solution to the problem.

I have to admit that I had my doubts about the PhotoReading whole mind system. But when I got into an involved conversation with our $40-an-hour consultant about computer networks (a topic I had known virtually nothing about two months ago), and never once lost track of what he was saying, I knew something was working!

My supervisor was with us at the time, and his jaw literally dropped when he realized that he was paying an outside expert so much to do what someone he had in-house could do. He offered me the job, and I took it.

Thank you so much for bringing this into my life!

Wyatt Camp

We live in the age of the accountant, not the poet...

...in the age of the politician, not the singer, in the age of the administrator, not the explorer. We thus live in an unbalanced world. Any development which redresses this imbalance is to be welcomed and applauded.

The PhotoReading Whole Mind System, initially developed by and now presented in written form by Paul R. Scheele, represents an excellent advance in redressing this imbalance. Paul's contribution has a number of noteworthy aspects to it. In particular, his work represents

• a practical system for achieving an important class of accelerated learning skills.

• a significant refinement in the extremely important and ubiquitous activity of reading—in particular, Paul has decomposed reading into a continuum of choices. By so doing he has, in effect, identified and charted a continuum of cooperation between the two cerebral hemispheres. This places within the grasp of the well intentioned and disciplined practitioner a set of choices which are the natural (and largely unrecognized) heritage of every member of our species.

• the presentation of a highly learnable system which both delivers what it proposes and simultaneously opens a huge door to achieving a new balance between unconscious and conscious processes within the user.

Well done, Paul Scheele!

John Grinder
Co-Developer
Neuro-Linguistic Programming

Of all the attempts I have made to improve my reading, this is the only thing that has made a significant difference and significant is not a strong enough word.

M. Curtis

PhotoReading works. It not only affects your reading, it also affects other areas of your life.

M. Tappin

PhotoReading is essential in today's information age and today's fast-paced world. It is a wonderful tool and learning process.

C. Bruha

I've rediscovered the joy of reading!

A. Preves

PhotoReading is probably the best tool I've found to unlock my potential.

S. Ritchie

This is not just about reading. It is about excelling in every area of my life.

C. Ogilvie

I wish I would have been able to learn this years ago.

R. Ochran

I've become more relaxed and am finally reading books which have been on my shelf for years.

P. Horoshak

PhotoReading changed studying from a chore to a pastime.

K. Pederson

The
PhotoReading
Whole Mind System

by Paul R. Scheele

Learning Strategies Corporation
900 East Wayzata Boulevard
Wayzata, Minnesota 55391-1836
612-475-2250 • 800-735-8273

Published by
Learning Strategies Corporation
900 East Wayzata Boulevard
Wayzata, Minnesota 55391-1836 USA
612-475-2250 • FAX 612-475-2373

Learning Strategies Corporation is a Private Vocational School licensed by the
Minnesota Department of Education.

"PhotoReading" is a registered servicemark of Learning Strategies Corporation.

"Paraliminal," "Personal Celebration," and "EasyLearn" are trademarks of
Learning Strategies Corporation.

Cover design by:
MartinRoss Design
1125 Xerxes Avenue South • Minneapolis, Minnesota 55405 • 612-377-5138

"The whole mind is represented on the cover. The analytical left brain is depicted
in the 19th Century French diagram of the planets revolving around the sun and by
the eyes of Albert Einstein. The creative right brain is expressed in Michaelangelo's
eye of David. Einstein's eyes suggest a want to look upward, to search further. The
type going off in space reflects the new learning strategies of the PhotoReading
whole mind system."

Illustrations by:
Jill Walz
5333 Bloomington Avenue South • Minneapolis, Minnesota 55417 • 612-729-1131

Library of Congress Catalog Number: 93-079859

ISBN 0-925480-50-9

Copyright 1993 by Learning Strategies Corporation

ALL RIGHTS RESERVED WORLDWIDE.

Printed in the United States of America
First printed in November 1993

10 9 8 7 6 5 4 3 2

How to Read this Book

This book is uniquely designed so that it is easy for you to read it in whatever amount of time you can commit right now.

25 Minutes (Level 1) - You can get the gist of this book in just 25 minutes. First, page through the entire book and read the table of contents, chapter titles, and subtitles. Page through the book the second time and scan for cartoons of Einstein riding a bicycle. Read the paragraph next to each bicycle cartoon. If you have more time, continue to Level 2.

30 Additional Minutes (Level 2) - You can absorb the core concepts of this book well enough to discuss them in just 30 minutes more. Page through the book again. This time scan only for cartoons of Einstein jogging. Read the paragraph next to each jogging cartoon.

45-90 Additional Minutes (Level 3) - You can fully understand the skills explained in this book by spending up to 90 more minutes. Page through the book one more time. Scan now for cartoons of Einstein with a light bulb over his head. Read the paragraph next to each cartoon. As you search for cartoons, remember what you have read before by reviewing titles and subtitles.

When cartoons are connected by lines, read all the paragraphs. Occasionally a note under a cartoon may say "Read Bullets;" this means you should read upcoming text which start with a bullet (•).

Resist temptation to read all paragraphs next to all cartoons during the first time you scan through the book. Comprehension will be higher if you go through the book more than once.

You may desire to read this book word-for-word the first time. That is all right. You may choose different levels for subsequent readings to help you get more out of your investment. Enjoy!

How to Use Our Telephone Support System

If you need more help learning any part of the PhotoReading whole mind system you may call a special telephone number.

Telephone icons with numbers are in two places in this book and in the quick reference guide at the end. These icons, such as the one on the left, indicate you can call to hear a recorded message designed to help you in your learning process.

You may listen to the recorded messages over a 30-day period for a subscription fee of $25. To subscribe, you may mail a check to Learning Strategies Corporation or call with a credit card. The address and telephone number is on the book's title page. (You may request a refund within 10 days if the service does not meet your expectations. Additionally, you will receive a $25 certificate which is usable should you decide to enroll in a PhotoReading class.)

You will be given a special telephone number and a secret 7-digit personal identification number (PIN) to be used only by you. You will pay normal long distance telephone charges on all calls. The subscription period begins with your first call to the system.

The number in each icon indicates the program you may select. When you call in, you will be asked to enter your PIN by using the key pad on a touch tone phone. You will then be asked to enter the two digit program number.

After the program, you may either hang up or enter another program number.

You will also notice fax icons throughout the book. These indicate additional materials that can be faxed to subscribers. Merely enter the program number just as you would to listen to recorded messages. If you call from a fax machine, the faxes can be sent immediately. You may also enter the telephone number of the fax machine you wish to receive the faxes.

Sample

Table of Contents

Foreword

Welcome to the most innovative reading program available. PhotoReading goes beyond mere speed reading. It is an educational experience that taps your mind's vast resources. It explores and expands your own potential.

We live in an age when too little time and too much information compete. If we are to succeed, we require new skills for processing and learning from information. PhotoReading is about working with the greatest information processing device known to mankind: the human mind.

In this book you will learn techniques for using the powers of your whole mind. PhotoReading will teach you not just how to read faster but *learn* at speeds many times faster than before.

When you learn PhotoReading, you will experience what might sound impossible. You will "mentally photograph" the written page directly into your other-than-conscious mind. There the information connects to your prior knowledge.

With the PhotoReading whole mind system you will develop extraordinary communication with your other-than-conscious mind. PhotoReading bypasses the limited capabilities of the conscious mind and helps you find your personal genius.

In **Part One**, you will overview the PhotoReading whole mind system and the new choices you have available as a reader.

Part Two guides you step-by-step to learn the PhotoReading whole mind system.

Part Three helps you integrate your new knowledge and skills so you can successfully use them every day.

PhotoReading is a triumph over information overload for thousands PhotoReading course participants worldwide. Now, the details of this system are explained in an easy-to-read format.

Acknowledgments

PhotoReading evolved dramatically in the last several years. I want to acknowledge the people who influenced its evolution. First on my list are my business partners **Pete Bissonette** and **Bill Erickson** who helped build Learning Strategies Corporation into a place where this remarkable system of human performance could flourish.

Patricia Danielson, president of Accelerated Learning Institute of New England, first enrolled in the PhotoReading course back in 1986. She soon earned certification as our first PhotoReading instructor outside Minnesota and has been leading PhotoReading courses ever since. Patricia worked closely with me to further develop PhotoReading. Her contributions to PhotoReading worldwide are numerous and sincerely appreciated. I especially acknowledge her integration of syntopic reading with the PhotoReading whole mind system and her efforts to insure classroom effectiveness.

Special thanks go to the many talented and insightful **associates** who have contributed to PhotoReading including Peter Kline, James B. Erickson, Lynette Ayres, Jean-Damien Valance and Eric Siegrist, Jerry Wellik, Dale Schusterman, and Charlotte Ward.

Certified PhotoReading instructors are a rare breed of educators. They influence PhotoReading by creatively exploring new dimensions in the classroom. Thank you to them all.

The most important contributor to PhotoReading is the **PhotoReading student** whose insights and breakthroughs are invaluable to PhotoReading's continued evolution.

Sponsors, support staff, and **marketing associates** also deserve acknowledgment. Without them this incredible program would be sitting on a shelf someplace collecting dust.

Doug Toft worked with me to synthesize years of writing about PhotoReading into the first manuscripts of this book. Thanks to Doug's early direction, the average person can read this book in two evenings.

Finally, I acknowledge **you, the reader,** for recognizing you have the power within to accomplish most anything you desire. People like you make breakthroughs such as PhotoReading a reality.

Paul R. Scheele

Part One:

Increase Your Choices

1

The Origins of PhotoReading

PhotoReading at 25,000 words per minute means you could "mentally photograph" this book in less than three minutes. Although this may sound like a radical new idea, the concept has existed hundreds of years before I coined the term PhotoReading. You can find evidence that such mental processing is possible and has been used in diverse settings from military training and martial arts to ancient religious traditions.

The challenge is not in deciding whether PhotoReading is possible. The challenge is how to effectively teach PhotoReading to anyone who wants to learn it. How can we transfer this natural ability into daily applications for reports, journals, newspapers, books, or whatever you want to read?

My background in neuro-linguistic programming and accelerated learning allowed me a way to meet that challenge. Now PhotoReading is taught around the world, and the time is right to share PhotoReading with you. The story that follows is how it all happened.

As a child, my passion for learning showed up everywhere except in the classroom. I learned mechanics from pulling apart bicycles, electronics from salvaging radios, leadership on the playground, and music in my rock 'n roll band. Even now I still explore my world with child-like wonder, and traditional education still seems incompatible with real learning.

Humiliating experiences with reading in school made learning from books a slow, confusing exercise—one to avoid as much as possible. On the rare occasion that I actually read for personal pleasure I always enjoyed it, often to my surprise. Yet, reading remained so laborious that I hardly ever did any.

Seven years after graduating with a science degree from the University of Minnesota, I took a speed reading test. I scored 170 words per minute at 70 percent comprehension. I was embarrassed when I realized my sixteen-plus years in public schooling left me below average in reading skills and an expert at putting off reading.

I thought that to read properly I must start on the first word of a text and slog through to the end. I must concentrate on seeing all the words correctly, make sense of them as I go along, and remember what they said. I also believed the ultimate measure of my reading effectiveness was total recall and critical analysis of meaning.

I did not question my definition of reading. I felt stuck at slow speeds. I knew that the faster I read, the worse my comprehension became. After seven years of professional life as a human resource development consultant, I made no improvement in my reading skills.

In 1984, the logical solution meant enrolling in a speed reading course. After five weeks of training, my speed reading scores were 5000 words per minute at 70 percent comprehension.

During one of the class sessions, a young woman sitting next to me lamented being stuck at 1,300 words per minute through ten weeks of classes. I suggested to her, "imagine what it would be like if you could break through to higher speeds now." On her next book her speed reading reached over 6,000 words per minute with higher comprehension test scores than ever before.

As great as that sounds, speed reading did not appeal to me. Pushing my eyeballs down the page soon became unrewarding drudgery. Three months after leaving the course, I rarely used the techniques but remained intrigued about the mind's potential for processing written words.

I began realizing my problem—I felt trapped between two opposing belief systems. One belief came from the elementary education model of reading. An opposing belief came from knowing that the human mind can achieve far more magnificent results. The same trapped and confusing feeling grabbed me once during private pilot's training.

I remember when my instructor took me up to 8,000 feet and told me to fly at a minimum airspeed just as I would when landing.

To do so, I slowed down the engine and pulled back on the control yoke to maintain my altitude.

Soon, the nose of my plane pointed almost straight up. The wind flowing over my wings no longer created enough lift to hold up the airplane. It could not fly so it dropped out of the sky like a rock, diving straight down toward the ground.

Terrified, I immediately began pulling back on the control yoke, trying desperately to get the nose up and fly the plane. This made things much worse. My instructor seemed to enjoy watching my panic.

Why wasn't it working? Why wouldn't the plane fly? Diving toward the ground at an accelerating rate, my instructor calmly said, "Push forward."

I knew he did not have a clue about our problem. While I tried to lift the plane up by the control yoke, he was telling me to dive deeper into the ground? Obviously he had lost his mind.

The plane entered a tail spin, and the earth became a spinning blur rushing toward us. Every part of me resisted his command as he insisted more firmly, "Push into the spin!"

Finally, my instructor broke my white-knuckled grip. He pushed the control yoke forward, immediately smoothing out the wings and elevator section of the tail, causing correct wind flow and generating lift. Slowly he pulled back the control yoke as the plane once again started to fly, leaving my heart in my throat. Wow.

What connection does this have to reading? Throughout my life I read only as fast as I could comprehend the words on the page. Every time I went too fast to comprehend, I grabbed control and pulled back as a fear reaction. I was afraid I would fail as a reader if I did not understand everything. My attempted strategies to read better and faster only made things worse. I was caught in the spin, and reading felt like nose diving my airplane into the ground.

Have you ever wished for a mentor to come along and pull you out of a nose dive? I did. Unfortunately, I did not realize a larger, more powerful capacity of mind could solve my reading problem. Fortunately, miracles happen. Several events in the next few years shaped a new direction for me.

In the fall of 1984, I entered graduate school to study adult learning and human development technologies. I wanted to know how people learn most effectively. My company, Learning Strategies Corporation, was over three years old with many clients who could benefit from my studies. I was also strongly motivated to improve my own skills as a learner.

Among the many seminars and courses I attended, I heard about an instructor from a speed reading school in Phoenix, Arizona. The instructor had suggested a bizarre experiment to one of his classes. After flipping pages upside down and backwards to learn eye-fixation patterns, he instructed the students to take a comprehension test on the book, just for the heck of it. Their scores turned out to be the highest the class had ever achieved. Was it a fluke? The folks at the school hypothesized that maybe they were turning the page into a stimulus which is processed subliminally.

About the same time I heard that hypothesis, back in 1985, I attended a workshop with Peter Kline, an expert in accelerated learning. When I told him about my interest in researching breakthroughs in reading, he offered me a challenge. A client of his, IDS/American Express, wanted a speed reading application of accelerated learning. Suddenly, a consulting job, my master's degree work, and my passion for learning landed in one nice package onto my lap.

In the fall of 1985, I began background research into studies of subliminal perception and preconscious processing. Significant research evidence suggested humans possess a preconscious processor of the mind that can absorb visual information without involving the conscious mind. I experimented using the eyes and the preconscious processor in special ways with written materials. We dubbed the concept of "mentally photographing" the printed page *PhotoReading*.

I devoted my full time to designing a course based upon the accelerative learning model, expert strategies of rapid reading, the human development technology of neuro-linguistic programming, and studies on preconscious processing. Soon the PhotoReading course was born.

One of my experiments involved returning to the speed reading school I had attended. I asked the teacher for several books and tests. After PhotoReading one of the books at 68,000 words per minute, I demonstrated 74 percent comprehension using the same type of written test the school used a few years earlier.

Too good to be true? Maybe. If you compare it to reading or speed reading, it is too good to be true. PhotoReading, however, was neither. Something powerful was happening, and the school confirmed the result.

In January and February of 1986, I taught the first six experimental courses—one to IDS and five to clients of my company. Participants stood up during class to describe many immediate payoffs including reduced stress, startling improvements in memory, fluid reading skills, top grades on school tests, increased wins for salespeople and trial attorneys, and more.

Inspired by participants' excitement, I worked on refining the curriculum design, teaching materials, and marketing approach with my business associates. On May 16, 1986, the Minnesota Department of Education licensed Learning Strategies Corporation as a private vocational school after reviewing the PhotoReading course curriculum and our business practices.

Since those early days, PhotoReading instructors helped me turn the course into four days of life-transforming human development experience. It is offered all over the world. The purpose of this intensive program is to acquire new skills that increase your reading efficiency. As most graduates admit, however, the course transforms more than your reading skills.

The PhotoReading whole mind system clearly directs you to "push into the spin" and discover the natural genius that resides within you. This means you fly smoothly through information instead of spinning out of control. This book will help deliver the system to you in clear, step by step instructions.

A preview of what is to come

The five steps to the PhotoReading whole mind system include preparing, previewing, PhotoReading, activating, and rapid reading.

The system appears as a set of steps in sequence, although it is actually a set of options that can be used in any order appropriate to your needs. It actually models the strategies used by highly skilled readers.

The secret power in the system is not in the techniques, but in the shift in perspective the techniques engender. To use the system and achieve your goals, you must confront the compulsion to habitually apply inefficient strategies.

In the pages that follow, you will examine the limitations which bind you to your present capacities. You will gain ways to bypass the limited processing capabilities of the conscious mind and connect with your other-than-conscious mind where your natural genius resides. The simple behaviors you learn can be used right away.

> Throughout this book I refer to the other-than-conscious mind. I use this term interchangeably with the terms inner mind, paraconscious mind, and preconscious mind. Some authors might use subconscious mind or unconscious mind to describe similar concepts.

Right now, you can only imagine the good that can take place as you use more of your innate talents. Over the years of teaching PhotoReading to thousands worldwide, I have witnessed many personal and professional transformations. Here are a few examples:

• A high school student PhotoRead the dictionary repeatedly and dramatically improved her vocabulary score on SAT exams.

• An attorney uses PhotoReading to quickly locate vital facts in huge law books. Now, instead of spending half-an-hour in a typical visit to the law library, he spends three to five minutes.

• A technical writer PhotoRead a client's software systems manual before his initial meeting with the project engineers. He was able to talk knowledgeably about the system with only 15 minutes of preparation time.

• A computer service technician consistently locates key information in reference manuals within seconds.

• An attorney took three minutes to read a 300 page legal manual from the Department of Transportation. He instantly turned to the one paragraph in the text that included the information he needed to win a case. The state's expert witness in this case—who had been unable to find this paragraph—saw the attorney perform this feat and was stunned.

• A waste water specialist for E.I. Dupont had to read a three-inch stack of federal regulations from OSHA in preparation for a meeting. During a 35-minute flight to the meeting, he PhotoRead the documents. During the meeting, he correctly stated that OSHA would no longer accept water treatment data that was more than three years old—a technical point buried in the regulations he had just PhotoRead.

These few examples only begin to express the benefits. Our clients also say that PhotoReading helps them to write reports, pass critical exams, excel in school courses, finish degrees, sail through meetings, earn promotions, and do more of the reading they really want to do for enjoyment.

The only requirements for PhotoReading are a willingness to experiment, use new ideas, relax, and play. Then the full genius within you will be released. Become like a child—as you were before education got hold of you—naturally curious, wondering, experiencing, discovering—and a whole new world of easy reading will unfold.

Reading will become a new source of personal and professional power. Information reading, pleasure reading, studying, and exploring written materials will occur with new levels of effectiveness. The benefits offered by the PhotoReading whole mind system will help you create a new quality of life that will delight and surprise you.

The next chapter gets you set and ready to go.

A student improved his high school math grade from a D to a B in one semester. He said that PhotoReading math books must have given him ways to do problems better. Another student PhotoRead a variety of books before preparing a theme paper. The teacher wrote on her paper, "A+ Your writing style improved overnight. What did you do?!"

Several musicians have reported uses of PhotoReading music. They find that PhotoReading musical scores a day before first playing the music makes the first run through much easier—as if they have already practiced the piece.

An actress is better able to memorize her lines by PhotoReading the script first. She also says this helps create a better understanding of her characters.

A doctor of psychology from Mexico was asked to present her 20-page research paper to a conference in California. Because it was written in Spanish, she would have to translate the paper as she spoke. Although she was bi-lingual, she had always found it difficult to speak English from Spanish writing. She PhotoRead the Spanish-English dictionary several times the day and night before her presentation. During her speech she spoke fluently without any confusion whatsoever. She reported being relaxed and completely comfortable the entire time.

2

Old Reading Habits or New Reading Choices

Take a moment to paint a vivid mental picture of the kind of reading materials you encounter regularly. Among the possibilities are:

- Magazines
- Newspapers
- Trade journals
- Mail
- Memos
- Owner's manuals
- Training materials
- Reports
- Proposals
- Sales literature
- Specification sheets
- Reference manuals
- Non-fiction books
- Novels, poetry, and short stories

Quickly answer the following questions in your mind:

- How well do you comprehend what you read?
- How well do you remember what you read?
- What are your strong points as a reader?
- What is the one thing you would most like to change about the way you read?

Play with two possible scenarios for your future, based on how you read today.

Here is one we call the plight of the elementary reader:

You enter your office on a Monday morning greeted by stacks of unread memos, reports, manuals, and journals accumulating on your desk. Those piles of paper feel like a reprimand. Rather than face them, you stash them in a drawer. Out of sight, out of mind...sort of. You cannot help worrying that you have buried a vital idea or fact—some critical insight that could lead to a promotion or help you avoid an embarrassing mistake. As you plod through your daily round of meetings and phone calls, you tell yourself that you will get to all that reading...tomorrow.

The situation at home is similar. There are piles of untouched magazines, newspapers, and mail cluttering your living space. The prospect of hacking your way through it all seems distant, at best. How about your chance to read for pleasure—to enjoy those novels, biographies, and motivational books you have been saving for a special day? That day just keeps retreating behind deadlines, crises, and previous commitments.

Sometimes further training or education seems like the answer. You get excited thinking about the career advances and extra income that you stand to gain. One question that stops you every time: How would I ever get all that reading done?

Even if, by some miracle, you did conquer all those unread stacks in your life, you still face the challenge of remembering, explaining, and applying what you read. Faced with those odds, you put off reading another day and live in a state of confusion, chaos, and quiet desperation.

Is this scenario familiar to you? Are you trying to cope in the information age using reading skills learned in elementary school?

Now consider scenario number two, which we will call the joy of the PhotoReader:

You begin each work day with the information needed to make effective and timely decisions. Those old stacks of unread mail, memos, reports, newsletters, manuals, and journals have vanished.

Reading technical reports, a task that used to consume hours of your time, now requires only about 15 minutes per document. At the end of your day you look at a clear desk feeling ready for the following day.

This quality extends to your home life as well. You live a largely clutter-free life. Gone are the piles of untouched books, magazines, newspapers, and mail that once crowded your living space. You keep up with the latest daily news in 10-15 minutes a day. Now you consistently find time for novels, magazines, and pleasure reading which go beyond the immediate demands of your job.

Your advanced reading abilities erase old fears about further education and training. You take courses to complete degrees, gain promotions, learn new skills, expand your knowledge, and satisfy your general curiosity. You glance at course outlines knowing you can stay ahead of the required reading and perform with excellence. Often you can complete the reading for an entire semester of a college course during the week you purchase the textbooks. Class reading assignments during the semester feel like review of what you already know. The background reading of a half-dozen books for required papers takes only an hour or two.

Whenever you read, you do so with a sense of effortlessness and relaxation. Your conversation and writing is articulate, fluid and persuasive. You find it easier to win approval for your proposals because your recommendations are backed by solid evidence. People comment on the breadth of your reading and depth of your subject knowledge.

You finish your reading tasks with time to spare. You can absorb several books in the time it formerly took you to read one. You can extract what you want from entire magazines in the time you used to read one article. In a single sitting you pare down or eliminate your "to be read" piles. And with the extra time, you consistently complete the top-priority tasks on your to-do lists. In the process, you free up time to goof off as well.

Hold this scenario in mind for a few more seconds. Savor the resulting feelings of mastery and pleasure. Enjoy the extra time, money, and pleasure that reading adds to your life. Isn't that nice?

Decide your future now

One message I hope you will take from this book, above all others, is that you can choose which scenario is true for you. You can place yourself on a path to either of these worlds in a moment. You already possess the power to create either scenario, and it is imperative to decide and shape the future you want.

If this appeal to shape your destiny as a reader seems overly dramatic or silly, then consider a statistic: fewer than ten percent of the people who buy a book ever get beyond the first chapter. (Congratulations! You are already into Chapter 2.)

Many people who enroll in our PhotoReading course say they typically never make it beyond the cover of the books they buy. Instead, they simply accumulate or circulate books, magazines, brochures, mail, memos, and reports. The information in these materials could just as well be written in disappearing ink.

As you go beyond the opening of this book, you will discover a set of tools for gaining a new experience of reading. Use the tools, and you will find it within your power to make the ideal reading scenario come true for you. If you do not go beyond this chapter, your experience of reading will stay the same as it is today.

Break old reading habits

I know you want results, and you will probably try many of the techniques I suggest. However, achieving new results means more than trying new reading behaviors. You must adopt an alternative view of what reading can be.

Take everything you know about reading and **you have just defined the barriers to getting new results.** Elementary school reading imprints us all with a model of reading that limits our minds. This model or "paradigm" exerts tremendous power over your actions and your potential results.

Elementary reading is a fairly passive affair, often done without a clear sense of purpose. Have you ever spent ten minutes reading a newspaper article to discover it was a waste of time? That happens when you read passively.

It is also one-speed fits all; generally we plow through every type of reading material—from comic books to textbooks—at the same rate. It makes more sense to get the facts from a trade journal with different·speeds than you would use reading a novel for pleasure.

We feel pressure to get it right the first time with elementary reading. We expect to comprehend everything in one pass through the material. If we do not, we feel inadequate as readers. Musicians do not pressure themselves to play music from a score perfectly the first time. Why must we be perfect as readers?

Think about all the tasks we are supposed to accomplish in that single pass through a document: comprehend the structure, grasp the key terms, and follow the main arguments or plot events. On top of that, we must remember it all, critique it, and quote it accurately.

Faced with these kinds of demands, the conscious mind often becomes overwhelmed and can literally shut down. This is compounded when we feel anxiety, which happens when we come to the end of a paragraph and have no idea what we just read. Has this happened to you?

Becoming overwhelmed by too much information is easy in this age of information overload. Have you ever found your eyes moving down the page while your mind went off to a far away land? It is as if the lights are on, but nobody is home.

This leads to document shock—a short-circuit in your internal connections. Too much current coming over the lines sends the wiring up in smoke.

This breakdown at the conscious level slows the flow of information to a trickle when we read. The more facts, details, and other data we try to cram in, the less we recall.

> *The analytical, linear processor of the conscious mind can only handle seven (plus or minus two) bits of information at a time.*

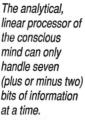

10

In this age of information overload it is easy to feel like a starving person with a can of soup but no can opener. With elementary reading skills, we often leave hungry: we plow through books, periodicals, manuals, and mail, only to find that we are craving something we cannot seem to get. Anything useful from these piles of information remains sealed from us.

Will elementary reading habits deliver what we need? If your answer is "no," you know the problem exists—and that is great. You have entered a powerful place, one where you are poised for change.

Embrace new reading choices

Readers who thrive today take a different approach than the elementary school model of reading. They are flexible in their reading. They adjust their speed to the type of material at hand. They know what they want from the written piece. They consistently find gems of information that deliver real benefit.

Active, purposeful, questioning and fully engaged—that describes the best readers. These effective reading strategies become a part of your repertoire as you learn the PhotoReading whole mind system. In the process, you will discover enhanced retention, recall and enjoyment.

> With the PhotoReading whole mind system you use the creative-intuitive mind as well as the critical-logical mind to accomplish your goals.

PhotoReading shifts you away from the prevailing elementary reading model into whole mind reading and makes you a blasphemer of traditional reading theory. As such you will encounter many people who will say PhotoReading cannot possibly work. The next story illustrates what I mean.

A colleague at Learning Strategies Corporation discovered that even college professors resist new paradigms. Faculty members at a college in Minnesota tried to block us from offering the PhotoReading course on the grounds that PhotoReading is impossible.

Feeling invulnerable, we agreed to offer a demonstration. A volume of U.S. patent law was projected, page by page onto a television screen. My colleague PhotoRead this material as it was displayed at approximately thirty pages per second (over 690,000 words per minute). Afterwards, he scored 75 percent comprehension. In addition, he drew approximations of six patent illustrations and correctly identified their numeric sequence.

The paradigm had shifted right before their eyes. Do you suppose they supported the course? No. Seeing is not believing. To shift your paradigm **you must believe it before you see it**. Think of PhotoReading as a paradigm shift, and you will do the "impossible."

You cannot "read" at 25,000 words per minute

Before learning PhotoReading, many people hear such stories as above and respond with, "That is nuts! There is no way you can read that fast."

They are right. No one's "conscious mind" can read that fast. PhotoReading is not "reading" as we know it. This kind of information processing is possible only when we temporarily bypass the critical, logical, analytical mind. We do not PhotoRead with the conscious mind. Instead, we draw on vast layers of the mind that remain largely unused during conventional reading. This literally means using the brain in a new way.

We still have to face everyday reading challenges, so let us employ an approach to reading that uses both hemispheres of the brain. From the left hemisphere we draw upon the abilities to analyze, sequence information, and reason logically. From the right hemisphere we get the abilities to synthesize, comprehend, create internal images, and respond intuitively.

When you learn to mentally photograph a book at a rate of one page per second—about 25,000 words per minute—you are taking a new approach to processing information. At such rates the old left-to-right, word-by-word, line-by-line method of elementary reading cannot operate. Instead, you meet the printed page using abilities ascribed to the right hemisphere of the brain.

After PhotoReading a book, the next step is to stimulate and activate your brain. This step of "activation" as we call it, lets you extract information you need from the book to accomplish your goals for reading.

Accepting that you can process the written word at an other-than-conscious level shifts the reading paradigm. Make this shift, and you can make your experience of reading powerful, effective, and easy.

Take an unexpected path to success

Some aspects of PhotoReading may seem whimsical at first. Instead of learning the expected techniques of speed reading, you learn about the tangerine technique, cocktail weenies, lucid dreaming and other unusual processes. I purposefully guide you through experience that you have not had, probably do not want, and do not think you need.

Sound odd? It is no more odd than discovering the principles of physics by learning how to downhill ski. Why not do it that way? To help the paradigm shift, we must take an unusual, unexpected path. Otherwise we tend to solve our reading problem in ways that fit our current view of the problem.

For example, when we have a lot to read, we tend to speed up...but our comprehension drops. We then slow down and overload the conscious mind. The net result is no increase in speed or comprehension but an enormous increase in internal conflict. This conflict recreates the problems we attempted to solve. And we still have a lot to read.

It takes away our excuses

If the thought of zipping through a book at a page per second sounds unlikely, remember that a new approach always seems outlandish when we view it through the lenses of the old model. When a paradigm shifts, everything begins again. Old rules may no longer apply. Even so, profound changes can happen painlessly, in an instant, and have far-reaching effects.

I like the way one of our PhotoReading graduates, a mechanical engineer, put it: "It is scary to think that our minds are unlimited. It takes away all our excuses." If you feel uneasy with the prospect of a paradigm shift, consider the words of another graduate: "Step into the unknown. Don't be afraid. You will either find solid ground, or you will be taught to fly."

We must try new attitudes and experiment with new actions. Otherwise, how can we produce new results in our lives? A person in one of our classes overcame his fear of success and said, "I finally understand. This course can transform my life—but I have been acting as though I can do it without changing any of my beliefs or my behavior!"

What you have to give up

Perhaps you have heard it said: *To achieve any goal you must be willing to give something up.* When achieving your goals in reading, the same rule applies.

To master PhotoReading you must give up:

Read
Bullets

- low self esteem as a learner
- self-defeating habits such as procrastination and self-doubt
- perfectionism, "all or none" thinking that dwells on failure rather than feedback and learning

- distrust in the inner mind and intuitive abilities
- the need to know everything right away
- performance anxiety
- a stressful sense of urgency

More than anything else, you must give up negative attitudes that get in the way of your success. For example, one participant in a PhotoReading class never considered himself much of a reader, and his belief became a personal barrier: "I just don't think I am going to be able to learn this." Another participant in the same class also claimed poor reading skills, but her approach was more open to giving up her limitations: "I am just going to do whatever it takes to master this."

Both people learned to PhotoRead. The first one, while clinging to a negative belief, found it much more difficult to discover the true abilities he possessed as a learner. When he made the important internal change, the PhotoReading whole mind system helped change his results in life.

As profound as PhotoReading can be to your life, there is an added reassurance: you do not have to give up any pleasure in reading. In fact, you get to keep your regular reading skills. A woman who loved reading novels exclaimed after taking PhotoReading, "I've rediscovered the joy of reading!" Her pleasure reading became a richer, fuller experience.

Here is the system

The demands placed on you as a reader in our age of information are tremendous. The PhotoReading whole mind system can help you meet any challenge. It works with any subject matter and flexibly adapts to different purposes, print formats, rates of speed, and levels of comprehension.

The five steps of the PhotoReading whole mind system use the abilities of your whole mind with power and effectiveness. With it you can approach any type of material and confidently get what you need.

Let us overview the steps now. In the next five chapters you will develop skills to apply each step effectively.

Step 1: Prepare

Reading effectively begins with a clear sense of *purpose.* This means consciously stating a desired outcome for reading. For example, we might want a brief overview of main points. We might want to gain certain details such as the solutions to specific problems. Perhaps we want to complete a task and seek only the ideas that will help us do so. Purpose acts like a radar signal to the inner mind allowing it to produce the results we seek.

Empowered with a clear purpose, we then enter a state of *relaxed alertness*—the accelerated learning state. While in this state, neither boredom nor anxiety exist. We are exerting effort, but we are not worried about results. Have you ever watched young children as they play? They model the same relaxed yet purposeful state we seek here.

Step 2: Preview

Our next step is to *survey* the written material. At this stage, our aim is not to grasp the content in detail, but to get a sense of its structure. To accomplish this with a book, we scan the outside cover, table of contents, the index, glossary, back cover, and any part of the text that stands out visually such as headlines, bold type, and words in italics.

During this step you also gather a list of key terms or *trigger words* which embody the core concepts or events. Trigger words alert your mind to the details you might want to explore more thoroughly later.

When done effectively, previewing is short and sweet—about five minutes for a book, three minutes for a report and as little as thirty seconds for an article. During that time we clarify and refine our purpose, *review* the trigger words, and decide whether to continue reading or call it quits. If you choose not to read something that does not meet your needs or interests, it is all right.

Previewing is based on an important principle: effective learning often takes place "from whole to parts." That is, we start

Read to end of chapter

with big vision of the whole thing and then proceed to the smaller more detailed parts.

Previewing is like x-raying a book—getting a broad sense of its underlying structure. Understanding structure gives us something that learning theorists call a schema—a set of expectations about what is coming up next. When we know the structure of written text, we become more accurate at predicting its content. As a result our comprehension and reading pleasure soar.

In summary, previewing gives us the skeleton of a book or article first. During the next steps of the PhotoReading whole mind system, you add body to the skeleton.

Step 3: PhotoRead

The PhotoReading technique begins with placing ourselves more fully into the relaxed, alert state of mind and body called the accelerated learning state. In this state, distractions, worries, and tensions seem to fall away.

Then we adjust our vision for the *PhotoFocus* state. Here the aim is to use our eyes in a new way: instead of bringing individual words into sharp focus, we soften our eyes so that our peripheral vision expands and the whole printed page comes into view.

PhotoFocus creates a physical and mental window—allowing direct exposure of the incoming visual stimuli to the brain. In this state, we mentally photograph the entire page, exposing it to the preconscious processor of the mind. The exposure of each page stimulates a direct neurological response. The brain performs its function of pattern recognition, unencumbered by the critical/logical thought process of the conscious mind.

At a rate of one page per second you can PhotoRead a whole book in three to five minutes. This is not traditional reading. After PhotoReading, we may have little if any of the material in conscious awareness, which means we may consciously know nothing. The next steps create the conscious awareness we need.

Step 4: Activate

During activation we restimulate the brain—*probing the mind*

with questions and exploring parts of the text to which we feel most attracted. We then *super read* the most important parts of the text by scanning quickly down the center of each page or column of type.

When we feel it is appropriate, we *dip* into the text for more focused reading to comprehend the details. In dipping, we allow our intuition to say, "Hey, turn to the last paragraph on page 147! Yes, that is the one. The ideas you want are right there."

You will learn many activation techniques in this book, all of which access the deeper impressions established by PhotoReading. When you activate you involve your whole brain, connect the text with your conscious awareness, and achieve your goals for reading.

Step 5: Rapid Read

This final step of the PhotoReading whole mind system is closest to conventional reading and speed reading. While rapid reading, you move your eyes quickly through the text, starting at the beginning and going straight through to the end. You will take as much time as you need, feeling free to adjust your reading speed depending upon the complexity, prior knowledge, and importance of the material. Flexibility is key.

Rapid reading is significant, because it dispels the prime fear of many beginning PhotoReaders that they will forget what they have read, or that they never absorbed any of the text in the first place. Rapid reading directly involves the conscious mind and satisfies our need for clear comprehension of the content.

> Reading is really learning from written pages. When first learning to play a new piece of music or a new golf course, you do not expect to do it perfectly the first time. You will learn as you go through each part several times. The multiple read approach of the PhotoReading whole mind system duplicates the appropriate way to learn anything new.

Remember, this step takes place after the other steps of the system. Those steps make us increasingly familiar with the text. There will be times when you choose not to rapid read, because you have already fulfilled your needs.

With this overview in mind, you are ready to do it.

An office administrator helped bring PhotoReading into her company so that her department could learn new skills to survive the deluge of information they all faced. Several years later she was recruited by a large company into a prestigious executive position. The salary was many times greater than what she was making as an office administrator. She told her former boss that her career advancement was made possible by the reading and learning skills gained from the PhotoReading whole mind system.

A high school honors student was extremely pressured with tremendous amounts of homework. She was prone to tension headaches and suffered from chronic tension in her back and neck. After learning PhotoReading she discovered her mind's natural gifts did not have to be forced. Using the PhotoReading whole mind system, she began relaxing her way to success. For example, she finished a difficult reading assignment in social studies, one which normally took two hours, in just fifteen minutes. She maintained her honors status, her headaches went away, and she discovered there is life beyond homework.

Several PhotoReaders with strong eyeglass prescriptions have reported a shift in their vision impairment. Within a year after learning the steps of PhotoReading, their annual eye exams did not follow the usual course of increasing prescription intensity. In fact, they reported an actual reversal to a lesser prescription. In each case the optometrists doing the exam claimed such reversals are extremely rare.

Part Two:

Learn the PhotoReading Whole Mind System

PhotoReading
Whole Mind System

3

Step 1: Prepare

I perform better at any activity, from public speaking to fishing, if I am well prepared. Yet, I used to pick up a book or magazine and just start reading with no preparation at all.

Now I treat reading as a goal oriented activity. Preparing for a few moments increases my concentration, comprehension, and retention of what I read. Preparing may seem simple, but it is the foundation of effective reading. All steps of the PhotoReading whole mind system actually revolve around preparation.

Being prepared to PhotoRead is much more than getting the book out to read it. It involves stating your purpose and fixing your point of attention to enter the ideal state of mind.

1. State your purpose

Establishing purpose is hardly a new idea. Francis Bacon, the sixteenth-century English philosopher, said it well, "Some books are to be tasted, others to be swallowed, and some few to be chewed and digested; that is, some books are to be read only in parts, others to be read but not curiously; and some few to be read wholly, and with diligence and attention."

All reading ultimately serves a purpose, either consciously or unconsciously. When we state our purpose explicitly, we greatly increase the odds of attaining it. Purpose unleashes ability. Almost anything can be accomplished with a strong sense of purpose. Purpose is the engine that drives the PhotoReading whole mind system. This consideration comes before speed, comprehension, or any other concern.

Establishing purpose is power which can be felt emotionally and physically. Readers with a firm sense of purpose acquire new feelings about the act of reading. They sit as if they mean business. When you have strong purpose, your body becomes strong and alert.

Read italics only

Set your purpose by asking questions such as:

• *What is my ultimate application of this material?* What will I expect to do or say differently after reading it? Maybe I simply want to pass time or savor the experience of reading.

• *How important is this material to me?* In the long run, how worthwhile is it? Does reading this material create value for me? If so, what specifically is that value?

• *What level of detail do I want?* Do I want to emerge from reading it with the big picture? Do I simply want to be able to list the main points? Do I want to recall

Example of purpose: A human resource consultant went to the library to PhotoRead the corporate report on a prospective client before their initial meeting. Her purpose for the eight minutes she invested was to get a feel for the trend of the company, where they had come from, and where they were headed. Her goal was to get in sync with the corporate executives and relate her skills effectively to their present and future needs.

Example of purpose: A banker wanted to interface his new computer with his new printer. After hours of trying, he remained unsuccessful. Before going to bed, he PhotoRead both manuals. His purpose was to let his inner mind work out the details of the problem and solve it upon awakening. Within the first half-hour after awakening, he had the printer working perfectly.

specific facts and other details? Is reading the entire document relevant to my purpose? Could I gain what I want by reading a single chapter or section instead?

• *How much time am I willing to commit right now to satisfy my purpose?* Making a time commitment gently forces attention on the task. I am increasing the importance of reading, because it is the only thing I choose to do right now.

In summary, do you want a general understanding of information, or do you need subtle details? Do you want to study something, or just gain pleasure and relaxation?

Too many people are on a trip with no destination. They approach reading with no sense of where they want to go. If I do not get value from what I am reading, I ask, "What is my purpose?" Invariably the answer is a resounding "Huh?" If I do not have purpose, my reading is passive and often wasteful.

Purpose and time management are inseparable. In the information age, we can no longer presume to read every document at the same speed or level of comprehension. Not only is this impossible given the amount of material we need to read, it is not even desirable. As Francis Bacon put it, some things are worth reading in great detail, others are not worth reading at all.

Keep in mind that your purpose can be quite inventive. For instance, your main purpose for reading in the dentist's office may be distraction: you simply want to avoid thinking about the sound of the drill in the next room. That is a legitimate purpose and prompts a distinctive experience of reading.

State your purpose every time you read. This habit engages the mind and increases concentration. When you establish your purpose, the full power of your mind comes into play.

In addition, purpose loosens the grip of guilt, a word that frequently arises when people talk about their reading habits. Many of us were imprinted with strict rules about how we are "supposed to read." One man said, "I bought the darn magazine, so even if I don't want to read all the articles, I am compelled to finish the whole thing."

With a sense of purpose, you can justify putting aside the material you do not need to read. Simply weed out the publications that fail to create value for you.

Establishing purpose takes as little as five seconds, yet the payoffs can save you hundreds of hours over the course of your lifetime. This technique is so far-reaching that it can instantly and permanently change the effectiveness of your reading.

2. Enter the ideal state for reading

When I read most efficiently, my body is relaxed and my mind is alert. If I maintain relaxed alertness, I am more able to comprehend, retain, and recall what I read.

To help you quickly and easily establish the ideal state of relaxed alertness, you can use the "tangerine technique." This simple technique automatically directs your attention and immediately improves reading performance.

Studies show that both reading and memory require attention. You can consciously attend to seven, plus or minus two, different bits of information at one time. (That is why Ma Bell originally made phone numbers seven digits long.) In other words, you have approximately seven units of attention available at any moment.

Research also indicates that fixing one unit of attention on a single point helps you effectively focus your other available units of attention when reading. Where you fix your point of attention is important. For example, when driving a car, the best point of attention is down the road—not on your hood ornament or the bumper on the car in front of you. For the efficient reader, the ideal point of attention is just behind and above the head.

The tangerine technique helps locate and maintain the ideal point of attention and instantly creates the relaxed, alert state of body and mind we desire for reading. Here are the steps to follow:

Read Bullets

• Hold an imaginary tangerine in your hand. Experience the weight, color, texture, and smell of the tangerine. Pretend that you have a tangerine and can weigh it with one hand. Now toss it into the other hand and catch it. Toss the tangerine back and forth between your hands.

• Now catch your tangerine in your dominant hand and bring it to the top back part of your head. Touch that area gently with your hand. Imagine feeling the tangerine resting there while you bring your arm down and relax your shoulders. You can pretend this is a magic tangerine, and it will stay in place no matter where you put it.

• Gently close your eyes and let the tangerine balance on the back of your head. Notice what happens to your physical and mental state as you do this. You will feel relaxed and alert. With your eyes closed, imagine your field of vision opening up.

• Maintain the relaxed feeling of alertness as you open your eyes and begin reading.

Here is an experiment you can do now to discover the potential effects of the tangerine technique. Take any page of this book you have not yet read. Without the tangerine in place, read two or three paragraphs. Afterwards, reflect on your experience. Then, put the tangerine in place using the method described above, and read two or three new paragraphs. Compare your experiences.

During the experiment, you might be overly self-conscious of doing something different. If so, you might find the effect hard to detect. Many people report a wider visual field, fluid movement of the eyes with less staccato or jumpy movements, and the ability to read word phrases or even whole sentences at a glance.

Playing with this technique lets you flow through reading material with increased speed and ease. Your ability to concentrate on the information improves, and reading becomes more relaxing.

At first you will consciously place the tangerine on the back of your head. Soon it will become automatic so that whenever you approach reading materials, one unit of attention fixes into place.

This physically relaxed and mentally alert state is also perfect for other important activities. It is widely researched as a state of peak human performance. This state is similar to contemplation, meditation, and prayer in which you are absorbed in the present moment.

While this is a state of relaxation, it is not the same as going to sleep or becoming drowsy. Rather, you focus your mind with an inner calmness. You have access to all your natural, inner resources.

Put it all together

The following procedure can help you prepare for reading in 30 seconds. You may wish to have a friend guide you through it or record it on tape so that you can play it back later.

*Read
Bullets*

• Place your reading materials in front of you. Do not read them yet.

• Begin to relax by closing your eyes. Become aware of yourself from head to toe. Your spine is erect, your posture is comfortable, and your breathing is relaxed.

• Mentally state your purpose for reading. (For example, "During the next ten minutes I will read this magazine article for ideas to help me improve my time management skills.")

• Place the imaginary tangerine at the top back part of your head.

• Become aware of yourself as relaxed and alert. Bring a slight hint of a smile to the corners of your eyes and the corners of your mouth to relax your face. Even with your eyes closed, you can imagine your visual field opening up. You have a direct eye-mind connection.

• Now, at a rate that is comfortable for you, maintaining this state of relaxed alertness, gently open your eyes and begin reading.

More on the tangerine technique

The ideal state for reading is typically in short supply for many people, especially at work. When we read at work, the phone is often ringing, someone in the doorway is talking, we have to hurry to make a meeting, and extraneous thoughts about groceries or car repairs keep a traffic jam in our heads. With such a morass of mental events, where does our attention end up? All over the place. Reading is next to impossible.

In contrast, the ideal state for reading is the flow state, when you are totally absorbed in the task at hand. That is where the tangerine technique comes into play.

In the mid 1980s I read a fascinating article in *Brain/Mind Bulletin* about Ron Davis, a reading specialist. Davis had dyslexia, a reading disability. While searching for a solution to this problem, he made a discovery.

People with dyslexia, he found, have a roving point of attention, one that wanders through space without coming to a fixed point. Skilled readers, on the other hand, have a fixed point of attention located just behind and above the top of the head.

By training himself to redirect his attention, he raised his reading, writing, and spelling skills from an elementary to a college level in less than three years. Today Davis runs a private clinic for people with learning disabilities. His sessions begin by training his clients to find this point, which he calls the "visuo-awareness epicenter."

I tried his technique myself and immediately noticed an increase in my concentration and ease in reading. If this technique had worked on dyslexics, I speculated, what might the effect be on a normal adult reader who has been too scattered to read efficiently.

Davis's work had provided me with a creative leap. To accomplish the effect of his "visuo-awareness epicenter," I developed the tangerine technique.

Most people find that several benefits flow immediately from the tangerine technique. To begin, they quickly and easily enter a relaxed state of alertness. In addition, they calm their minds and automatically focus their attention. The result is an instant improvement in reading skills.

Historically, the tangerine technique has come down to us in a variety of forms. The Chinese thinking cap, the wizard's cap, and even the original concept for the "Dunce cap," believe it or not, were all devices for focusing attention. Each causes part of your attention to fixate at a place above and behind your head.

Experiment with this technique. If the image of a tangerine does not work for you, then try another way of fixing your attention to the place above and behind your head. Imagine wearing a sombrero, with a bird sitting on top of it. Feel the sombrero resting on your head and focus your attention on the bird.

Another way is to imagine standing outside of your body, looking over the top of your head as you read. As you do this, there is a noticeable shift in the way you feel.

When you fix your point of attention with any of these techniques and open your eyes, a curious thing happens. Suddenly, the material you are reading seems more manageable. Your visual field enlarges, and you can even see your hands holding the pages. In this state, you are prepared to take in far more visual information than before.

Your state of mind is the important thing. We are not trying to hold the feeling of a tangerine the entire time we are reading. Getting a fixed point of attention is much like setting a keystone at the top of a stone archway. The one stone at the top holds all the rest of the stones in place.

Similarly, the one fixed point of attention seems to gather and focus the other units of attention to the task of reading. Once you have placed it there, forget about it. When you pass through a doorway, you do not have to carry the doorway with you. Just go ahead and begin your reading—your mind will take care of the rest.

Read Bullets

Take a moment to think of how you can use what you have learned in this chapter:

- Preparing is the foundation to the whole mind system.
- The two components to preparing are stating your purpose and getting into the ideal state of mind with a fixed point of attention at the top, back part of your head.
- Reading purposefully means reading with power.
- The tangerine technique is one way to fix your attention which automatically leads to the ideal state of mind.

Give yourself a few moments now to apply this technique to the remaining chapters of this book. Visualize yourself reading the rest of this book with strong purpose. Imagine shifting your attention to a point just behind you and on top of your head. Again, notice the shift in your physical state when do so. As you read, you feel more relaxed, centered, attentive, and fully absorbed. Now you are poised at the flow state, ready to learn. Your next step is to...

PhotoReading
Whole Mind System

4

Step 2: Preview

We can only read what we already know. That is, the human brain can only comprehend patterns that are familiar. The more you know about a text before you actually read it, the easier it will be to read.

The fast track to discovering patterns within text is previewing. It speeds your comprehension and only takes a few minutes or, in some cases, a few seconds. There are three stages to previewing:

1. Survey the written material
2. Pull out trigger words from the text

3. Review and decide your goals for going further

1. Survey the material

When my wife and I considered purchasing our home, we first explored the neighborhood. We walked to the lakefront and around the block, and we drove to the elementary school and into town. We looked at a map and explored the nearby county and regional parks. In other words, we surveyed the territory.

As you consider reading a book, magazine, or other publication, survey it too. You will learn its structure and know how to proceed. Walk around the written material to notice:

*Read
Bullets*

- titles and subtitles
- table of contents
- copyright date
- index
- text printed in boldface or italic print, including headings and subheadings
- text on the front and back covers
- first and last pages of books, or in other documents the first and last paragraphs of any sections
- material set off as boxes, figures, or charts
- summaries, previews, or review questions

You may be amazed at how much you can gain through this strategy. In some cases, you will find everything you want to know—just through surveying.

Surveying allows you to know what the text seems to be about and can help you predict what to expect. It can help direct you where to look for important information.

"How to" books, for example, usually present you with a number of tasks to perform in a certain order. A "what is" book often presents a problem and offers a solution.

Do not spend much time surveying: a short article, 30 seconds; a longer article or report, three minutes; and a book, five to eight minutes. That is all. If it takes any more than that, then you are probably reading in a conventional sense—not surveying.

Surveying has an added advantage. It promotes long-term

memory, because it helps you comprehend and categorize the material you read. It encourages you to build a mental structure of what you read. Any material you actively organize, you will remember longer.

2. *Pull out trigger words*

Have you ever felt while reading that certain words were leaping off the page and begging for special attention? Chances are those important words are the focal points of the author's message. Those words have an urgency. "Hey, look at me," they seem to say. Those words are trigger words.

Trigger words are key words—the high visibility, repeatedly used terms that present central ideas. They are the handles which will help you grasp the meaning of a text.

Trigger words help the conscious mind formulate questions for the inner mind to answer. Your other-than-conscious mind tends to highlight them in its search through the text as it helps you accomplish your purpose.

Locating trigger words is simple. Chapter 2 of this book offers an example. There I mention elementary reading, paradigm shift, purpose, and beliefs. Those terms qualify as trigger words describing a problem and ways to solve it.

Most people locate trigger words with ease when it comes to non-fiction. They might draw a blank when previewing fiction such as short stories, plays, novels, and poetry. Fiction offers us trigger words in the names of persons, places, and things.

Locating trigger words is a fun way to test the waters before diving for meaning. Just flip through every 20 pages or so of a book and notice what words catch your attention.

All places you survey will aid your search: table of contents, covers, headings, and the index. In an index, look for the words that are followed by the most page numbers. These are bound to be important trigger words.

At first I suggest that you make a mental note of five to ten trigger words for an article and write a list of twenty to twenty-five trigger words for books. You should be able to reach those numbers in two minutes or less.

Be playful and relaxed, and it will be easier to fixate on high powered terms.

3. Review

The last part of previewing helps assess what you have gained from your survey and list of trigger words. Take a mini-inventory. Determine whether you want to go farther with the document and extract more of its content. Think about whether you can meet your purpose for reading or whether you need to re-define that purpose.

Remember the 80/20 rule? Ask yourself whether this book or article relates to your "top 20 percent."

> The 80/20 Rule:
> If all items are arranged in order of value, 80% of the value would come from only 20% of the items, while the remaining 20% of the value would come from 80% of the items.

After previewing, you might even decide not to read the document. That is one of the kindest things you can do for yourself in this age of information overload. Save yourself the trouble of ingesting information you do not need. You have other things to do. Save time for them.

After previewing, you might decide you only need to know the document in a general way. Later, if you want more specific information, you will know where to find it. It is like using a set of encyclopedias: you do not have to memorize the contents of each volume. You only need to know enough to pull the correct volume off the shelf.

Read as you would shop for groceries

Your brain excels at classifying perceptions and recognizing patterns. Previewing helps accomplish both. It allows you to build meaningful categories, establish patterns, and locate the core concepts which lead to understanding. You start to discover the four to eleven percent of the text that includes its key message and satisfies your purpose.

Without categories, the text would appear as the world does to a newborn—a constant parade of unrelated sights, sounds, and other sensations, a "blooming, buzzing confusion," as psychologist William James described it.

The secret to successful previewing is to avoid getting into a text too deeply too soon. You may find yourself tempted to stop previewing and start reading for details. Notice your urge to focus on the particulars, let that urge go, and return to previewing.

You want to get the maximum benefit from every minute you invest in reading. If you start reading for details too soon, you could easily end up slowing down, plodding through paragraphs and pages that have no relevance to your purpose. That could lead to the loss of momentum, waning interest, and even a wonderful nap.

To avoid this, hold back a little on the details. This strengthens your motivation. It creates a desire in you to find out more, to fill in the general structure that you are building in your mind.

That is one of the juiciest parts of previewing—getting hungry for information and ideas. That hunger increases your commitment to reading and energizes the whole mind to achieve your desires.

Preview every time you read. Reading a longer or more complex document without previewing is like going to the grocery store to buy an apple and searching every item on every shelf until you find it. Instead, look for the fruit section and walk directly to what you want. When reading, this means taking a direct path to the passages that most directly satisfy your purpose.

In this chapter you learned:

• Previewing lets your mind create patterns to increase speed and comprehension while reading.

• To preview you must survey, pull out trigger words, and review.

Read Bullets

• Surveying is a walk around the outside edges of what you are reading in order to understand its structure and how to proceed.

• Trigger words are key terms that help you formulate questions which your inner mind will work to answer later.

• Reviewing is a mini-inventory that helps you make sure you are reading what meets your purpose.

To apply the technique of previewing, take a moment to imagine the types of reading materials you might face in the coming week. Imagine previewing those various sources of information. Notice how a few moments of previewing can save you hours of time this week, because you quickly tune into the information you want and eliminate the redundant and unnecessary reading you can fly past.

Chapter 5 brings you to the next next step, PhotoReading, the most provocative and exciting of all.

An executive said that PhotoReading dozens of books on management principles has improved his job performance. Another received an unusually large pay raise a year after the PhotoReading class—she said she developed such an increased understanding of the industry through PhotoReading that it dramatically improved her productivity.

A minister PhotoRead a section of the Bible before sleeping one evening. He dreamed about a Bible story and how it related to a problem in the life of one of his parishioners. He was able to use his insights to counsel the parishioner.

A businessman was asked to speak at a conference. He was unable to prepare for the presentation in the traditional sense of reading books, taking notes, and writing his speech. He was only able to PhotoRead several books, so he figured he could wing it. To his surprise his presentation flowed with aplomb. He even presented statistics which just popped into his head—apparently provided by his other-than-conscious mind. Later he verified every fact with the books and received excellent feedback from his audience.

A computer programmer learned that by PhotoReading pages of code, he quickly discovers program bugs. Another programmer said his ability to write effective code improves when he PhotoReads pages of code written by other programmers.

A chemist discovered that PhotoReading his college text books helped develop his understanding of charts which in the past presented problems.

5

Step 3: PhotoRead

PhotoReading will knock your socks off! It is the most right-brained and provocative step of this system. To master it, you have to keep a playful and open-minded attitude.

PhotoReading relies on the brain's natural ability to process information at a preconscious level. For those who let go and trust their mind to do the work, PhotoReading provides a phenomenal opportunity to discover their true potential for learning.

Through PhotoReading, you expose your brain to patterns of text by mentally photographing the printed page. This is not a technique to work hard at or something which can be consciously understood. To strain at practicing and perfecting it may be counterproductive. Just use it—and enjoy the results.

During the next few pages you will learn the ways to perform each step of the PhotoReading process. After learning them, play with PhotoReading this book.

1. Prepare to PhotoRead

Preparing yourself for PhotoReading is a matter of making a few decisions. What is it you want to PhotoRead? Place your reading material in front of you and ask yourself if you can spare the few short minutes required to PhotoRead it.

Why do you want to take the time to PhotoRead this material? Clearly state to yourself what you expect to get from the

> There are six steps to the PhotoReading process. In order they are:
> 1. Prepare to PhotoRead.
> 2. Enter the accelerative learning state.
> 3. Affirm your concentration, impact and purpose.
> 4. Enter the PhotoFocus state.
> 5. Maintain a steady state while PhotoReading.
> 6. Close.

materials. This act of establishing your purpose will be repeated more precisely later in the process. Purpose is essential.

Choose to remain attentive to this experience and let go of any outside interferences. Be in an open posture, comfortable, upright, relaxed, and ready to enter the accelerative learning state.

2. Enter the accelerative learning state

Earlier in the PhotoReading whole mind system, you entered a state of relaxed alertness before previewing. Before PhotoReading, your aim is to experience a more receptive brain state—a state in which you have access to expanded capabilities of mind and increased readiness to learn.

Here is a procedure for entering this state, also called the accelerative learning state. At first, this procedure might take several minutes to complete. Eventually, however, you will reach the desired state in the time it takes for one deep inhale followed by a gentle exhale.

• Make yourself comfortable. When you are first learning this technique, lie down. After that, sit back comfortably in a chair.

• Take in a deep breath. Exhale, and then close your eyes.

• Experience full physical relaxation. Take in a deep breath and hold it for a moment. As you exhale slowly, think of the number three (3) and mentally repeat the word "relax." This is your physical relaxation signal. Then progressively relax the major muscle groups of your body from head to toe. Imagine a wave of relaxation flowing throughout your entire body. Let each muscle melt until it is

pleasantly relaxed and free from tension.
- Now calm your mind. Take in a deep breath and hold it for a moment. Exhale slowly, thinking of the number two (2) and mentally repeating the word "relax." This is your mental relaxation signal. Let go of thoughts about the past or future. Focus your awareness on the present moment. As you breathe out, let any tensions, anxieties, or problems float away. As you breathe in, let peace and tranquillity flow into every part of you.
- Take in another deep breath and hold it for a moment. Slowly exhale, mentally hearing the sound of the number "one" (1). As you do so, picture a beautiful flower in your mind's eye. This signals that you have focused your awareness and entered the resource level of mind—a state of expanded creativity and ability to learn.

Imagine yourself in a beautiful, quiet place. Become aware of the soothing sights, sounds, and feelings you experience there. Imagine that an hour of time is elapsing. Let yourself rest comfortably there for a few moments.

Before you proceed to the next steps, gently remind yourself to release any remaining tension or distractions. Remind yourself to maintain this state of physical and mental relaxation as you PhotoRead.

Brain states are characterized by subjective experiences and electro-encephalagraph (EEG) frequency measures (Hz stands for Hertz or cycles per second).
Waking state = 12-23 Hz, Beta.
Relaxed alertness, optimal for learning = 8-12 Hz, Alpha.
Deeply relaxed, good for internal imagery, associated with creativity = 4-8 Hz, Theta.

The above process of entering the accelerative learning state allows you to establish contact with your other-than-conscious mind. Entering this physical and mental state turns on the brain's right hemisphere and opens it to input. It allows you to be more responsive to your own positive ideas. While in this highly attuned state, you open up access to the deeper "data base" of your long-term memory.

Many classes, books, and tapes on relaxation and meditation can help you gain skill at entering the ideal learning state. The Paraliminal Tapes available from Learning Strategies Corporation guide you through similar relaxation techniques used in PhotoReading classes.

3. *Affirm your concentration, impact, and purpose*

Thoughts either support or derail the learning process. Positive, affirmative thoughts assist learning, and negative thoughts prevent it.

Placing positive thoughts in your mind can help you develop skills and achieve desired results. These thoughts, called affirmations, help direct the material you PhotoRead into your inner mind. The most useful affirmations for PhotoReading include:

Read Bullets

- As I PhotoRead, my concentration is absolute.
- All that I PhotoRead makes a lasting impression on my inner mind and is available to me.
- I desire the information in this book, (say the title here), to accomplish my purpose of (restate your purpose).

Affirmations give direction to your other-than-conscious mind by clearly establishing goals. The process of affirming also bypasses the limitations imposed by the conscious mind. It redirects any negative internal dialog and opens you to the possibility of success.

It is important that your goal or purpose be one you can achieve. A poorly formed goal would be "I want to have photographic recall of everything I PhotoRead." Since that is not the purpose of the PhotoReading step, and perfect recall of everything is not reasonable, such an ill-formed goal could lead to undue frustration and non-performance.

A well formed goal would be, "To fully absorb this material and to speed my application of these techniques and concepts in my life." The achievement of such a goal is within your control and leads to greater ease and success.

4. *Enter the PhotoFocus state*

The PhotoFocus state uses your sense of sight to input visual information directly into the other-than-conscious mind. In this step, you learn to use your visual system differently than with regular reading. Rather than hard focusing on individual words and word groups, you achieve a "soft gaze" to notice the entire page at once.

When I first developed Photo-Reading, I knew that hard focusing the eyes sent information through the conscious mind. PhotoReading required sending information through the preconscious processor into the inner

> With PhotoFocus you strengthen the eye-mind connection. You shift the emphasis from the page in front of your eyes, to its meaning which is stored behind your eyes (in your mind).

mind. My question became, "How can I look at something without using hard focus to look at it?"

De-focusing the eyes was not the answer. That only made me feel spacey and lethargic. My feelings of relaxed alertness vanished as if my physical and mental clarity was connected to my visual clarity.

One afternoon I mulled over this paradox. I read an article about an art teacher named Betty Edwards. In her book, *Drawing on the Right Side of the Brain*, she said, "If you want to draw my thumb, don't draw my thumb," because you will use the left brain—the analytical, non-artistic side of the brain. She said, "To draw my thumb, draw the space around my thumb." That strategy uses the right brain—the creative side of the brain.

Using her advice, I began looking at the two pages of an open book. I took in all the white space in one expansive gaze, not looking at the words. Suddenly, the pages took on a clarity and depth, appearing almost three dimensional. In the center of the page there emerged a third, rounded narrow page.

This reminded me of experiences I had as a child. My mind tended to wander if I had to sit and wait. Occasionally, if I happened to be sitting in a room with a tile floor, I became aware that the floor appeared as a three-dimensional grid—as if there were two layers of lines, about six inches deep. If I tried to look at it, it would disappear. The effect would only linger if I maintained a relaxed, divergent gaze, as if looking into the distance.

The recognition of this unique visual state was the beginning of PhotoFocus. In the years since then, many discoveries have connected PhotoFocus to ancient traditions of seeing with the other-than-conscious mind.

The essence of PhotoFocus is using your eyes in a new way which is called "seeing with soft eyes." This contrasts hard focus which is our normal practice of getting a sharp, clear image of a single word, phrase, or line of print. With PhotoFocus we open up our peripheral vision and prepare to mentally photograph entire pages at once. In so doing, we process visual information at a preconscious level and feed it directly into the deeper memory of the inner mind.

> *Seeing with "soft-eyes" is hardly new. Taoist literature from China refers to an "all-seeing gaze." So does Carlos Casteneda, author of a popular series of books about the practices of Don Juan, a Mexican shaman.*

A clear description of soft eyes comes from Miyamoto Musashi, a legendary fifteenth-century swordsman and author of *The Book of Five Rings*. In that book, Musashi refers to two types of vision. One he calls ken, an observation of surface appearance and external movement. Kan, in contrast, is seeing into the essence of things. Using the peripheral vision of kan, said Musashi, a warrior could spot an enemy and detect an impending attack before it happened. Though we have no enemies to attack, with PhotoReading we can use the other benefits of kan: calmness, concentration, creativity, intuition, and the ability to greatly expand our visual field.

The physiology behind kan—or PhotoFocus, as we call it—is fascinating. The retinas of our eyes can be divided into two regions. One is the fovea which is densely packed with cells called cones. These cells bring images into hard focus. Each cone has a single nerve connecting it to the brain. Information entering the fovea is processed by the conscious mind.

As we move into the periphery of the retina, the second area, we find different cells called rods. Even though several hundred rods are connected to the same nerve, these cells are extremely sensitive. In fact, they can detect the light of a single candle ten miles away. While in the PhotoFocus state, we are drawing much more upon rod vision than cone vision. The periphery of our visual field is processed by the other-than-conscious mind.

Using PhotoFocus, you reduce your perceptual defenses and eliminate interference from the conscious mind. Removing these blocks to incoming information will help you access more of your inner mind.

An example of such a block is tunnel vision. It can happen when you are looking for something in the kitchen. It may be right there in front of you, but you do not see it because you are expecting it to be in a drawer, not on the counter.

As a preparation for entering the PhotoFocus state, play with the following exercise. The aim is to experience a visual phenomenon I call the "cocktail weenie effect."

To see the cocktail weenie effect, find a spot on the wall to look at. Now, while continuing to look at the spot, hold your hands about eighteen inches in front of your eyes. Then bring the tips of your index fingers together.

As you gaze at the spot just above the top of your index fingers, notice in your visual field what is happening to your index fingers. Keep your eyes relaxed and do not worry about bringing anything into sharp focus.

You may notice a ghost image that looks like a third finger, as in the following diagram:

That ghost image looks like a cocktail weenie.

This might seem like child's play, but in reality it signals a significant change in your vision. Seeing the cocktail weenie demonstrates you are diverging your eyes instead of converging them on a fixed point of hard focus. When you do this, your visual field softens, and your peripheral awareness expands. It is strange that you will see the effect only when you do not look at your fingers. I am asking you to see it without looking at it? That sounds like something from Kung Fu.

You can apply the same effect to the pages of a book. To experience this, fix your gaze on a point comfortably beyond the top of the book. Notice the four edges of the book and the white space between the paragraphs while gazing just over the top of the book at your spot on the wall. Because your eyes are diverging, you will see a doubling of the crease between the left-hand and right-hand pages. Begin to notice a little rounded strip of a phantom page (cocktail weenie page) between the crease lines. I call that page the "blip page."

See if you can move your gaze down from over the top of the book, so that you are looking right through the center of the book as if you had x-ray vision. Can you maintain divergent eyes and still notice the blip page?

In the early stages of learning PhotoFocus, many people discover that their eyes try to focus on the book. This causes the crease lines to converge, and the blip to disappear. That is the power of habit. Do not fight it. Just relax and play with it. You may want to leave it and play with it again later.

When in PhotoFocus, the print on the page is probably blurred. That is okay, because to see the blip, you must place your focal plane at some distance away. To have clarity up close, you will need to relax your eyes and have the focal plane move in.

When you develop PhotoFocus, there is a unique clarity and depth to the words on the page. They are not in focus, because you are not looking at them. But there is a clarity to the print that you can notice as you relax more.

Rand
Dot
Stereo
gram

Here is another way to see the blip page. Sit back from a table just a bit. Place your open book on the table near the edge. Look past the bottom edge of the book and see your feet on the floor. Slowly move the book into your visual field so that it almost covers your line of sight to your feet. If you notice the book in your visual field, you will probably realize that there is a doubling of the crease in the book.

As you keep looking down at your feet, notice what is happening between the two crease lines of the book. That is the blip page.

Play with moving yourself more toward the book (and the book more toward you) until your line of sight is right through the center of the book, and you still have the double line. Can you do it? If it is tough, do not worry. After years of habitually focusing on the printed page, your first exposure to PhotoFocus might be challenging. Then again, you might find this all quite easy.

What happens if you do not see the blip page? No problem. You have not failed. In fact, you can still be a proficient PhotoReader. Just use another method for gaining PhotoFocus: looking at an open book, right at the center crease, open up your field of vision so that you see all four corners of the book. Soften your gaze so that the lines of print are not in hard focus. Instead, notice the empty margins and the white space between paragraphs. Imagine an "X" connecting the four corners of the book. (Use this technique if you are sighted in only one eye.)

As you experiment with these techniques, go easy. Remember, hard work does not help. Relaxing and noticing your experience are the main ingredients of success. After playing with your visual system for two or three minutes, just close your eyes and rest for a few minutes before you play again.

Many of these exercises can help strengthen and balance your visual system. Since all natural eye improvement methods are based on relaxation, it is important to give yourself the chance to rest your eyes.

The point of these exercises is not to hallucinate but to teach yourself how to diverge your eyes. Achieving "soft eyes" and maintaining PhotoFocus while PhotoReading will take time, so be patient.

The ideal posture for Photo-Reading is sitting upright, with the book propped up at a 45 degree angle to the table (90 degrees to your eyes). Your gaze will be through the center of the book, but at first, it is okay if you gaze over the top in order to see the blip. If you cannot maintain the blip at first, it is better to go with noticing the four corners and the "X", rather than struggling with divergence.

5. Maintain a steady state while flipping pages

Your accelerated learning state and PhotoFocus state may be fragile at first. Distracting and self-critical thoughts may disrupt your attention, and you might find yourself tempted to bring the printed page into hard focus again. If this happens, simply remind yourself that your purpose right now is to maintain an ideal state for learning. Place the imaginary tangerine on the back of your head (refer back to Chapter 3), and notice the blip page again.

You can use two additional techniques to maintain your state while PhotoReading. First, keep your breathing deep and even. Second, chant to the rhythm of the turning pages. These actions occupy your conscious mind, keeping it free from distractions while your other-than-conscious mind continues PhotoReading. The chant—a rhythmic internal statement of supportive words—is particularly important, because it focuses your mind and blocks negative thoughts that might otherwise occur.

Maintaining a steady state will enable you to breeze through books quickly and effectively. The steady rhythm is wonderful for keeping the brain relaxed and open while you mentally photograph the pages.

Here is how to maintain the accelerative learning state while
PhotoReading:

Read
Bullets

- Remain in an open posture. Rest your feet on the floor, and
keep your arms and legs uncrossed.
- Keep your breathing deep and even.
- Turn the pages of the book in a steady rhythm—one page
every second or two. See every two-page spread with "soft eyes."
Your gaze is through the center of the book, noticing the blip page.
If you cannot see the blip, notice the four corners of the book, the
white space on the pages and an imaginary "X" connecting the four
corners.
- Chant to the rhythm of your turning pages. Take one flip
for each syllable of the following chant as you mentally repeat:

Re-lax...Re-lax...
Four-Three-Two-One...
Re-lax...Re-lax...
Keep the state...See the page...

- Do not concern yourself with missing pages. Just let them
go. You can always come back to them on a second pass through the
book.
- Continue the chant to the rhythm of your page turning. Let
your conscious mind follow the words of the chant.
- Let go of distracting thoughts by bringing your conscious
mind gently back to the activity at hand.

6. Close the process with a sense of mastery

There is a natural tendency for the conscious mind to question
what it gains from PhotoReading. If you tell someone you just
PhotoRead a book in three minutes, the first question asked is,
"What can you tell me about it?" A comedian joked about speed
reading, "I just read *War and Peace*. It is about Russia."

Such a statement simply indicates that you receive little or
nothing at a conscious level while PhotoReading—which is largely
true. Unfortunately, it also implies that nothing was gained at a
deeper, other-than-conscious level. This easily becomes a negative,
self-fulfilling prophecy. Statements such as "I won't remember a
thing" or "This can't possibly work" act like requests to your deep

mind to forget what it gained while PhotoReading. If you continually make such statements, you will find that they become fulfilled.

To prevent this situation, close your PhotoReading session by taking charge of your thoughts and setting the stage for activation. Remember that the other-than-conscious mind makes no judgments about the information it processes. Now is the time to request that your mind integrate the information and make it available for future use.

After PhotoReading, your mind immediately begins processing. It does so spontaneously at an inner level, below the threshold of conscious awareness. The information has made an impression on your inner mind and will be processed as you instruct your mind using affirmations.

Affirmations which we use in our classes include:

• I acknowledge the feelings I have received from this book...and...

• I release this information for my body and inner mind to process.

• I am curious as to how many ways my mind can demonstrate that this information is available to me.

Your response to the material you PhotoRead occurs within you. These affirmations invite your inner mind to help. It is fun to consciously recognize the many ways this information can become available.

If you like, you can imagine a bridge between your conscious and inner mind along which the information flows. As you let go and relax even more, you can more easily notice whatever flows into your conscious awareness.

The six steps of the basic PhotoReading procedure are easy to put together. Do not let their simplicity deceive you. This technique can have a profound impact on you.

A fascinating warning

With PhotoReading you blast information through your nervous system in a powerful way—like drinking water through a fire hose. Be open, let it digest and absorb at an other-than-conscious level. To do so, relax and let go. But watch out, there is a warning we have offered over the years.

Make sure the last book you PhotoRead before sleep contains information of a positive nature. A client who took the PhotoReading course made the mistake of PhotoReading *War & Peace* and *Les Miserables* before going to bed. She claimed, "I tossed and turned until three in the morning and had one of the worst night's sleep of my life."

The inner mind reviews information during the sleep state that has been taken in below the conscious level of awareness. Studies dating back to the early 1900s show that such information can have quite an effect on one's dreams. Since this is going to happen, you may as well make sure you PhotoRead books before going to sleep that will be gentle to your mind.

Now you have learned the six steps to the PhotoReading process. In order they are:

1. Prepare.
2. Entering the accelerative learning state.
3. Affirm your concentration, impact and process.
4. Enter the PhotoFocus state.
5. Maintain a steady state while PhotoReading.
6. Close.

Read Numbers

If you have not tried it yet, take a few minutes to PhotoRead this book, or before you go to sleep tonight PhotoRead another positive and uplifting book.

After you have prepared, previewed, and PhotoRead, you are ready to bring the knowledge you desire into your conscious awareness as you Activate in Chapter 6.

A high school English teacher used the PhotoReading whole mind system to prepare for an American literature unit on Hemmingway. She PhotoRead all the commentaries on Hemmingway's writing, plus all other Hemmingway books including the two the class unit would cover. In addition, she rapid read the two books. She surprised herself with her ability to teach. Her knowledge on the subject gushed with rich examples giving the class depth that surpassed any unit she had ever taught. She remarked that the material activated spontaneously during her lectures.

A mother PhotoRead her children's homework to effectively help them with their studies.

A law student gave the PhotoReading whole mind system the ultimate test. During the first semester she PhotoRead all her assigned readings and used the system as recommended to activate whenever time permitted. She always kept on top of her studies, contributed in class, maintained a relax and confident attitude, and achieved top grades on four hour essay exams which she completed in just in two hours. During the second semester, she went back to her old reading and study methods to find out what difference PhotoReading makes. After just two weeks she called off the experiment declaring that her old study skills created more work, misery, and feelings of overwhelm.

A graphic artist routinely PhotoRead design books. He said it heightened his creative ability.

A proofreader discovered that after PhotoReading documents first, she missed fewer mistakes.

6

Step 4: Activate

A professor at a state university in Minnesota had been asked to give a speech. Most of what he wanted to present was contained in two books, so he PhotoRead them at bedtime, expecting to activate them the next day.

That night, he dreamed of delivering his speech. As he awoke from his dream, he grabbed a pencil and paper and jotted down everything he could remember of his dream/speech.

In the morning, he reviewed his dream notes and realized his speech was completed, save a few transitions which he added. Later that day he examined the books and discovered his notes contained all the relevant points he needed.

I love hearing such stories from PhotoReaders. Those examples are great when they happen. For most beginning PhotoReaders those experiences are the exception rather than the rule. You and I need to know that we can consciously access the information we need from materials we PhotoRead. We cannot just sit back and hope we will dream about it at night and be ready to speak before a group or perform on a school test.

Activation, the next step in the PhotoReading whole mind system gives you the conscious awareness needed to fulfill your purpose. Through the process of activation we build increasing levels of conscious comprehension. You begin gaining awareness, move to a sense of familiarity, and finally achieve the knowledge you desire.

> Four levels of comprehension:
> 1. Awareness
> 2. Familiarity
> 3. Knowledge
> 4. Expertise

Activation after PhotoReading is quite different than trying to recall what you read in a regular manner. Activation techniques are designed to restimulate the new neural connections you created by PhotoReading, rather than trying to force recall through the critical/logical conscious mind.

Being active and purposeful is essential for gaining conscious comprehension. During activation you are attracted to text relevant to your purpose. If you have no purpose for reading a document, there is generally little benefit that can be gained from activation.

There are two types of activation: spontaneous and manual. *Spontaneous activation* occurs without conscious effort on our part. Perhaps you have had the kind of "aha!" experience that happens when you suddenly solve a problem that has occupied you for weeks, or see the face of a friend in a crowd, or remember the name of someone you met months ago.

Such activation is an automatic connection to past experiences, to neural patterns already existing in your brain. There are stimuli in our environment, cues we may have not been looking for, which spontaneously trigger a flood of previous associations. Spontaneous activation feels similar to a flash of creative insight—sudden and unexpected.

Although there are many stories of spontaneous activation from PhotoReading course graduates, they remain the cherry on top of the whipped cream dessert and are not the main entree of the PhotoReading whole mind system.

Manual activation which we will describe in this chapter means to activate by design. It uses the actual text as a catalyst for restimulating the brain, bringing the information you need into consciousness.

As you learn to activate, notice what you are feeling, doing, and thinking when experiences of awareness, familiarity, or knowledge occur. This careful observation will help you understand your own intuitive signals and further your activation skills.

Wait before activating

The first step of activation is an act of creative procrastination. It is another one of those paradoxes: in order to comprehend your reading, let it go while it incubates in your mind. Wait at least 20 minutes, or if you can afford the luxury, overnight.

The concept of initial effort followed by a period of incubation and rest is well known to writers, artists, musicians, and scientists. The secret is to distinguish incubation from inactivity. Your other-than-conscious mind never sleeps. It is on the job 24 hours each day—when you sleep it creates dreams, generates solutions to that gnawing problem you face at work, connects your current thoughts to a vast network of associated prior knowledge, and so on.

Let what you PhotoRead take its place in your brain, becoming part of the neural network. Activation will then cue up the associations your brain has constructed. You consciously connect, meet your needs, and satisfy your purpose for reading.

A PhotoReading instructor told me a story of how easily the mind can use activation to accomplish reading goals. "I was teaching a class in the city where my daughter lives when a participant shared a poem with the word *serendipity* in it. That evening, I wanted to look up the word when I was at my daughter's house. I walked into her den and went into PhotoFocus as I asked myself, 'What is here that will help me?' I hadn't even finished stating the question when my arm reached toward the bookshelf and grabbed a book. The book happened to be one my daughter had borrowed five months earlier. At that time I had never read it, so before she took it I had spent five minutes PhotoReading it, figuring I would never see it again.

"It all seemed like an odd coincidence, so I just let the book open on a page. And there on the bottom right corner of that page was Webster's definition of the word 'serendipity'."

Obviously the other-than-conscious mind has a sense of humor. What more perfect way to explain what serendipity means than by giving a serendipitous experience. The point is, if we ask, it shall be given unto us.

Probe your mind

After your brief hiatus, be it 20 minutes or 24 hours, begin activating by asking questions. For example: what is important to me in this book, article, or report? What are the main points? What is in here that can help me? What do I need to know to perform well on the next test, to write my report, contribute in the next meeting, etc. Queries like these send a probe to your deep mind, opening a channel to the answers you desire. They stimulate a sense of curiosity, opening channels for information flow. Mind probing causes the inner mind to begin finding the best ways and means to your goal of comprehension.

It is important, as you ask questions of your mind, that you not expect an immediate answer. Expecting recall at this stage in activation creates frustration. When trying to recall information after PhotoReading, the conscious mind merely searches recent memory. Finding nothing in store, the conscious mind tends to shut off access to the vast database of the other-than-conscious mind. Mind probing initiates the process of building comprehension. You can stay open by staying curious.

Another powerful mind probing technique is discussing what you have read. Once you start summarizing a book or article, other people might get curious. They will often ask you questions about your reading—questions that encourage you to articulate the core concepts.

When you pose questions, make lists, or enter discussions regarding what you have read, you are making a request of your other-than-conscious mind. Such activities initiate a search through the vast database that lies just below your everyday awareness.

Ask yourself questions in a state of relaxed alertness, confident that answers can come, and with genuine curiosity. You will be pleasantly surprised at the results. The bridge between your conscious and preconscious data base becomes sturdier when you consistently probe your mind in this way.

Super read and dip

After probing your mind, you may want to know more from the text you are exploring. What else do you want to know? Where in the text can you go to find it? When super reading, the next step of activation, you quickly move through the text to retrieve the answers you seek.

First, you will turn to sections of the text which attract you in some way, based on your purpose for reading. There will be "visual cues" or clues in your materials that give you a sense that certain sections are more important to you than other sections. These clues may be chapter titles or sub-headings in the text that carry relevant information.

Then super read by rapidly moving your eyes down the center of each page in the section you have chosen. Notice that parts of the text attract you as being more important. At those sentences or paragraphs you will "dip" into the text, reading a sentence or two until you sense that you have received what you want from the passage. Then resume super reading.

In class we often explain super reading with a visualization that is straight from those sacred bastions of American literature—

comic books. Imagine that you are Superman coming to the Earth for the first time.

From an aerial distance of one hundred thousand miles, you see the Earth as a swirling blue ball. You set a flight path straight toward the planet. From ten thousand miles away you can start to make out the outlines of continents. You also notice how much of the planet is covered by water. Zooming in closer, you notice the variegated land surfaces: deserts, rain forests, prairies, and mountains.

Suddenly, you are attracted to a lush, green island with a sandy beach and a magnificent ocean view. You touch down, spend a short time exploring the terrain, and take a quick dip in the water. Satisfied, you take to the skies again, searching for another place to land.

This is a perfect metaphor for super reading and dipping.

Super reading allows you to soar over the whole printed landscape. Dipping allows you to touch down on the parts of text that directly serve your purpose.

How do you know where to dip? Just follow your hunches. Your brain has been exposed to the entire text by PhotoReading, so let your internal signals at the periphery of your awareness be your guide. Do not worry about justifying your decision every time you decide to touch down for dipping; those signals are pre-logical and pre-verbal. They come from your other-than-conscious mind. Monitor them and discover where they lead you.

You can use the same technique when locating anything, by the way—not just places to dip. There are many situations in life when you can draw upon the wisdom of the other-than-conscious mind.

My wife Libby went to an estate sale in which a roomful of old books were being sold. As she walked in, surrounded by floor to ceiling shelves full of books, she entered PhotoFocus. She asked herself, "Is there an old or rare book in here that Paul would want?" Her eyes instantaneously flashed over to one book which she walked across the room to pick up. It was the perfect book for me. Although her mind told her there were no others, she spent the next 20 minutes looking at every title, only to discover her mind was right—there were no others.

When super reading and dipping, follow your intuitive signals about where to look. Sometimes it is as simple as noticing where your eyes are pointing and choosing that direction. Sometimes you will find your hand just opens the book to the exact page. Pay attention. Notice whatever signals your mind offers.

Super reading and dipping, like all steps in the whole mind system, are strategies that keep you active, questioning, and alive to your purpose. You end up with enough information to make crucial decisions: where is the sentence or paragraph that sums up the essential point of this document? How much of this text is relevant to your purpose? Do you want to continue reading this or go to another source?

While dipping, you might experience a common problem. There is a tendency, because of years of schooling, to think we should dip into everything. If this happens, you are reading unnecessary details that do not serve your purpose. For example, you dip to read an illustration the author is making about an important point. That works. The next several paragraphs give additional, but redundant, illustrations. If you dip into those, you may just be wasting your time. If you waste too much time, you bog down in details and possibly veer off course into more irrelevant material.

That is when the old reading paradigm is often rearing its head. Your conscious mind may be on a guilt trip. For some of us it is as if our second or third grade teacher is reprimanding us by saying, "Stop! You missed a word. Go back over that more carefully. You are not really reading that. Now do it right!"

When you get these kind of signals, thank that part of you for its concern. Let go of the worry that you are missing things as you super read. Your grade school trained conscious mind wants you to read, comprehend, remember, and critique everything as you go. But reading experts for over fifty years have said that is the worst way to read. Keep in mind that comprehension comes in layers. Each time you super read and dip, you peel back another layer of "not-knowing" to reveal what you need at the core of your text.

Trust your intuition and dip when you feel strongly moved to do so. If you dip into information you do not need, remember the purpose for your reading. Tell yourself to look for the spot where that information is contained and dip there.

With a firm purpose, your vast, other-than-conscious mind is free to use its natural ability to bring you to the information you need. You are playing a new game, and messages of fear and guilt from the conscious mind only get in the way.

As Frank Smith points out in *Reading Without Nonsense*, making the effort to memorize the content as we read actually interferes with comprehension. Such readers are often worried about forgetting details as they read, and this anxiety blocks comprehension.

When in doubt, remember the vital statistic given by Russell Stauffer in his book, *Teaching Reading as a Thinking Process*. He claims that only four to eleven percent of the text carries the essential meaning. In fact, there is a common way to test the readability of a text for a particular audience: cross out four out of every five words. Then ask members of the intended audience to see if they can still sum up in a general way what the passage is about. If the text is written at an appropriate reading level, most audience members will be able to do this.

Here is a guideline for super reading and dipping. When you stop to dip, limit your dipping to a paragraph or two at a time for articles and a page or two for books. Going back to our comic book analogy, as Superman you can settle down, savor the scenery, and mingle with the locals later. Right now your overriding purpose is to keep exploring the planet, not to settle in on the island and live out the rest of your days.

In the scheme of the PhotoReading whole mind system, by the time you super read and dip, the text you are reading has become your friend. You are very much in a familiar conversation with the author, posing questions as you super read, and discovering the answers as you dip. This is one of the most playful and juicy steps in the PhotoReading system.

As a PhotoReader, you are on a crusade for ideas that can help you solve problems and raise the quality of your life. This is a dramatic quest worthy of any super hero or heroine.

As you make super reading and dipping part of your life, you may find ways to apply it beyond the written page. A jeweler who attends trade shows annually to purchase inventory decided to use the PhotoReading whole mind system to accomplish his goal at the trade show.

He stood at one end of the auditorium to get a panoramic view of the exhibits. He "PhotoRead" the entire place walking quickly down each aisle in a PhotoFocus state. He called to mind the kind of stones he was looking for to fill his store's inventory and began "super reading" as he walked down one aisle at a time. Whenever he got a clear intuitive signal to go to a certain booth, he obeyed it and "dipped" in there.

Following this method, he managed to find all he needed in two hours. In previous years, his old method of methodically searching aisles usually took five days to accomplish the same end result.

As you integrate the PhotoReading whole mind system into your life, you will automatically do things as the jeweler did. In this way PhotoReading becomes an all-purpose tool. It is more than a technique for gathering information from books.

Super read along the train of thought

When you super read and dip, go into the places where the payback will be greatest. Your brain is well trained by the time you are in ninth grade to know where to go in a text. It is skilled at searching for cues that lead to meaning.

For example, your brain knows that there are more visual cues in the upper half of our alphabet than in the lower half. Take a look at the following sentences:

~~Can you see what I mean about visual cues?~~
~~Do you find this easier or more difficult?~~

See? It is easier to make sense of the words when you see the upper half. Similarly, there are more cues for meaning in the topic sentence of a paragraph, than in the rest of the paragraph. And, in a five paragraph theme, there are more cues in the first and last paragraphs.

When activating an article or book, look for the cues that will give you the most meaning. Look at the structure of the written piece and determine the author's scheme for writing. Then super read and dip to follow the author's scheme.

Here is what I mean. Perhaps you know that the author first describes a problem, then later in the text explains how to solve the problem. Let us say you want the author's steps for solving the problem. Because you understand the author's scheme for writing, you can bypass what you do not need and move quickly to the place for dipping and achieving your goal.

We call this "following the author's train of thought." In the PhotoReading course I use an illustration to represent this:

• The problems the author grapples with drive the train.

Solution • main argument • problem

• The main argument about where the problems come from is the main "cargo" in the flow of information. This cargo is built upon certain propositions the author is trying to sell you and is composed of key terms.

- The solutions emerge to suggest a remedy for the problems.

The train of thought is one scheme used by authors to present information. Discover other structures within articles or books. These structures for presenting information show you where to super read and dip to quickly get the information you need.

One more point about super reading and dipping: though these strategies may sound like conventional speed reading, they are not. Super reading and dipping take place after you PhotoRead. In addition, the goal is not to memorize the material or make it all available to the conscious mind. Instead, super reading and dipping help you sense its structure, retrieve essential information, categorize the material in a meaningful way, and build a mental summary. As a result, your comprehension and long-term retention of the material increases.

Create a mind map

While looking through a box of my old graduate school materials, I discovered a wonderful contrast between two types of class notes. One type of notes was the traditional linear outline of everything the professor said—an endless series of unintelligible scratching. I remembered trying to decipher those notes while reviewing for tests; what a horrid chore.

The second type of notes was an alternative, highly visual set of colorful diagrams called "mind maps." They reminded me how fun it was to create and review class information. Looking them over brought back a flood of vivid details. Mind mapping, as it is called, had transformed my classroom experience forever.

Mind mapping is fast, highly efficient, and promotes long-term retention. It is an excellent way to activate and synthesize information after super reading and dipping.

Following is a mind map that sums up the five steps of the PhotoReading whole mind system.

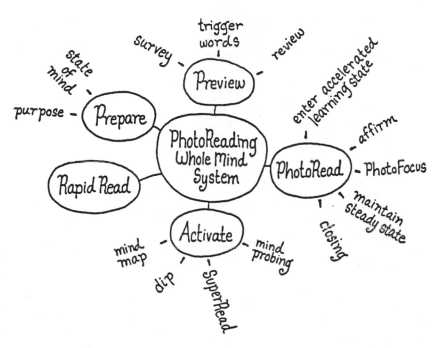

After looking at a few mind maps, you can deduce the basic
guidelines for this system:

• Put the core concept in the center of the page.

Read

• Write supporting concepts on connecting lines radiating

Bullets

from the center.

• Use key terms only—often they will be trigger words
identified in your preview. Express each concept in three words or
less.

• Include visual elements—cartoons, images, symbols,
icons—wherever they seem appropriate.

• Add color. In the above mind map, for example, all the
words pertaining to Step 1 could be written in one color, all those
for Step 2 in a second color, and so on.

Two of the best books on mind mapping explain this technique
in more detail. They are *Use Both Sides of Your Brain* by Tony Buzan
and *Mind Mapping* by Joyce Wycoff.

When mind mapping, you may also find it helps to use sheets

of paper that are larger than the standard 8-1/2 by 11 inches. If you do stick to standard-sized paper, at least turn the paper sideways so that you are writing on a horizontal frame. Most people find this gives them more room to record ideas.

Mind maps are highly individual. Your mind maps will look different than anyone else's, even if you are making notes on the same material. That is okay. Ideally, your mind map reflects your experience. The images and associations that promote your long-term memory are unique to you.

Following is another mind map of the whole mind reading system, illustrating a different format:

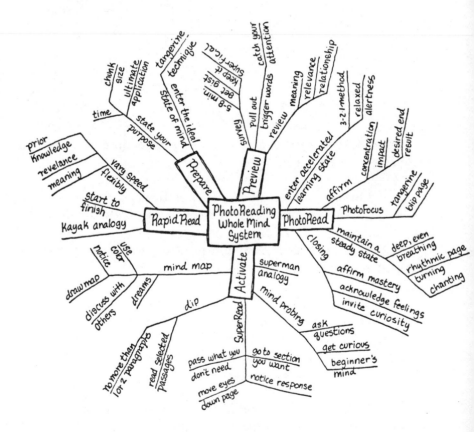

Even if it feels awkward at first, play with mind mapping as an activation exercise. Because mind mapping uses visual memory and spatial intelligence, it accesses the most powerful memory centers of the brain. Moreover, mind mapping mirrors the way the mind works—linking ideas by branching association rather than linear logic. Perhaps that is why mind maps begin to feel so natural so soon.

Gain a new experience of memory

This book is about shifting your paradigm of reading as a whole. To aid that process, we need to reconsider the role of memory.

In the last few years, I have become fascinated by the work of Gerald Edelman, MD, a Nobel prize winning neurologist and author of *The Remembered Present* and *Bright Air, Brilliant Fire.* Edelman's ideas offer the most convincing explanation I have yet found for what may be happening when we activate material we have PhotoRead.

Edelman's theory claims that memories are not stored in a localized fashion in the brain but are reinvented each time we access them. What happens when we remember is that we create a mental context for an idea, re-enter important cues or bits of related information, and follow neural "tracks" that have been laid by previous experience. When enough cues are entered and the correct neural pathways are stimulated, the ideas and images we want to "remember" are not recalled from storage but are recreated right on the spot.

Applying this view to PhotoReading and activating, we begin to understand what might be happening to produce such remarkable results. When we PhotoRead, the brain processes written materials more physiologically than cognitively. That physical exposure to the brain opens neural networks inside the brain that can lead to later mental connections.

The result is increased speed, familiarity, and ease of comprehension. You will have the ability to connect with the most important information almost instantly, rather than trying to figure it out as you read. You do not have to waste time investing hours in a book to get the knowledge you want.

This is much like laying a set of railroad tracks for a train to travel on later. PhotoReading lays in the tracks. When we activate the material, we re-enter the original information through super reading and dipping, and the conscious mind follows the tracks to the destination of full comprehension.

I admit I cannot do justice to Edelman's theory of memory in a few short paragraphs. It is far more important for you to experience this process rather than have me try to explain it. The activation techniques of mind probing, super reading, dipping, and mind mapping are all gateways to that experience.

In review of the ideas of this chapter, you learned:

• There are two types of activation: spontaneous and manual. This book is concerned with manual activation.

Read
Bullets

• Clear purpose is essential for activation.

• It is best to wait after PhotoReading before activating—at least 20 minutes, but ideally 24 hours.

• Mind probing, the first step in activation, means asking questions that you want to answer.

• Super reading and dipping involve moving quickly over sections of text that attract you, then reading selected passages that answer your questions.

• An understanding of the author's scheme or structure will help guide your super reading and dipping.

• Mind mapping is a highly visual and spatial way to take notes. It helps activate materials because it uses the whole mind.

• Activation stimulates the brain giving cues to the associations your brain has constructed. As a result, you consciously connect, meet your needs, and satisfy your purpose for reading

The final step of the PhotoReading whole mind system is Rapid Read which is presented in Chapter 7.

7

Step 5: Rapid Read

During the PhotoReading class I ask participants a question after we have prepared, previewed, PhotoRead, super read and dipped in a book: "How many of you would still like to get more out of this book?" Usually, 40% of them will raise their hands. Then I ask, "What specifically would you like to get out of the book?"

To this question several reply precisely. They know exactly which parts of the book they may want to study in more detail. For them, the next step is additional super reading and dipping to complete their goal.

Others shrug their shoulders and say, "I don't know, I just want more." This unspecified "more" is a signal for the final step of the system: rapid reading. The choice to rapid read is made when you know you want more from the text, and the laser-like precision of super reading and dipping will not bring you there.

Rapid reading is similar to accelerated conventional reading with two significant differences. First, rapid reading comes after all the other steps of the PhotoReading whole mind system. Second, the speed of rapid reading is highly flexible.

To rapid read, move swiftly through the text, taking as much time as you need. Go from start to finish without stopping. Feel free to vary your speed, depending on the complexity and importance of a particular passage.

You will read faster when:

• You have already read that paragraph or page during one of the other steps. You zip past it.

• You recognize that the information is simplistic or redundant. Since you already understand it, you zoom past it at super reading speeds.

• You quickly see that the section you are reading is unimportant to your purpose so you can flash past at PhotoReading speeds keeping your intuition open to stop you if it tells you to check something out.

You will read slower when:

• The text contains new information with which you are unfamiliar.

• You sense complex information which needs more careful consideration.

• You recognize an extremely important passage you want to explore in more detail.

The end result is that you move at varying speeds through the text: sometimes faster, sometimes slower depending upon importance, complexity, and your prior knowledge of the information.

An essential point in rapid reading is that you keep moving. Never pause to struggle with information you might not understand. It is common to stop when you do not fully understand what you are reading. That is part of the old paradigm. Instead, just keep reading.

If you stop and try to wrestle with what you do not know, you can get sidetracked and never finish. If you just keep going, soon you will come to information you do understand—discovering clues in the text which answer the questions you were stuck on previously. By staying in a relaxed, alert state with rapid reading you keep extracting the information you want—information that relates directly to your purpose.

Rapid read or super read?

A common question is, how does rapid reading differ from super reading? At first glance, the two steps might seem similar. Rapid reading, however, proceeds straight through the text, from beginning to end. Super reading, a step of activation, seeks out sections of the text you are attracted to and zips lightly down the center of the page.

Rapid reading might involve slowing down to a more conventional reading speed; you might do this to comprehend a technical drawing or mathematical formula, or to savor a line of poetry. In contrast, super reading means maintaining a brisk speed and dipping into the text at any point; there is no requirement to move through the pages in order.

Super reading has been compared to the actions of a Superman scanning the Earth from outer space and deciding to touch down on certain continents. We need another analogy for rapid reading— perhaps that of taking a river kayak trip. Sometimes you career over white water rapids, then paddle leisurely on placid waters. Then you might be back to rapids again. The point is that we stay active and alert, and our speed varies depending on the material we are covering.

Rapid reading is not always necessary. At times previewing, PhotoReading, and activating may be all you need to attain your desired reading outcome. Many business people never need to use the step of rapid reading. When reading business related information, such as reports and manuals, they achieve their purpose using the other steps of the system.

Students studying a textbook and people reading for pleasure will use rapid reading quite often, because it gives the conscious mind more to explore.

PhotoReaders who enjoy reading novels will preview, PhotoRead, then move directly into rapid reading, bypassing the activation steps altogether. Play with the wonderful options the PhotoReading whole mind system provides you. You will find the best path to achieve your purpose for reading.

How to prove the system works for you

The rapid reading technique is reassuring, because it builds full conscious comprehension of the materials you are studying. Like the manual activation techniques from the previous chapter, rapid reading works mostly with the conscious mind.

As you achieve your reading goals using the PhotoReading whole mind system, you might wonder which step is having the greatest impact upon your success. It will be easy to assume that the techniques involving the conscious mind are the biggest contributors, because when you use them you gain conscious comprehension. It will be difficult to think the other-than-conscious step of PhotoReading really did anything at all.

The system works because it is a *whole mind* system. Both the conscious mind and the other-than-conscious mind participate. By all means, enjoy the benefits you receive consciously. At the same time, keep noticing other positive effects in your life that we might assign to the domain of the inner mind.

The most stunning demonstrations of the PhotoReading step often come as spontaneous activation. Stories of spontaneous activation from PhotoReading graduates are wonderful encouragement to all beginning PhotoReaders. They all have similar characteristics.

The reports sound like this: "I was in the situation in which I needed or wanted some information, and it showed up. I was not even trying at the time to remember it. It just happened. The information just appeared, just popped into mind, not because I was trying to recall it, but almost on a whim."

The "aha!" experience of spontaneous activation is a convincing demonstration. It has been proof for many people that the PhotoReading step of the system was actually working for them. The paradox is, how do you plan to have a spontaneous experience? You cannot, because it must be spontaneous.

In lieu of a chance, spontaneous activation experience there are other ways to test the system. In my original studies of PhotoReading, I had very compelling evidence that PhotoReading was working. Some evidence came from spontaneous activation, but mostly it came from manual activation techniques.

For the first year of my graduate studies, I did not have the PhotoReading whole mind system. In the remaining eighteen months I used PhotoReading for everything. The contrast was enormous. I felt on top of every subject, completed reading assignments and research reports with ease. The pressures of keeping up with my studies vanished.

Since those early days of PhotoReading, I have consistently seen that students in school have the best ongoing demonstrations that PhotoReading works. Why? Because they are using and testing the system all the time, both objectively and subjectively.

If you are not in school, you need to set up your own measures. I want you to have a convincing experience of PhotoReading. Here are some ways you might test it for yourself:

- For one week, PhotoRead everything and activate anything which you feel you need to consciously comprehend. The next week, go back to regular reading. You decide which week was most productive.
- When you see a book at a friend's house that he or she has recently read, ask if it was worth reading and how long it took to read. Borrow the book and spend one-tenth the time with the book, using the five steps of the PhotoReading whole mind system. Then, get together with your friend and discuss the book, without mentioning that this is your own private test. Afterwards, let your friend decide if you understood the book.
- Before a business meeting, preview and PhotoRead five books related to the topic you will discuss at the meeting. Decide afterwards if your performance was unusual in any way.

All of these "tests" are easy, relatively low-risk, and explore uses of the PhotoReading whole mind system. Play with them and have a compelling demonstration of your own.

You do not have to stop here. There are many ways to extend the steps introduced so far. Use the suggestions in the remaining chapters to discover more applications for PhotoReading. Make it a skill you use daily for all your reading needs.

An attorney found himself challenging an expert witness during cross-examination without a clear sense of why he was asking the questions. It became obvious as the expert witness' testimony unraveled. The attorney had PhotoRead books the evening prior which contained facts contradicting those of the witness. At conscious level, the attorney did not know the facts. From an other-than-conscious level, his mind had given him the guidance necessary to achieve his goal.

An entrepreneur had difficulty understanding the advice of his legal consultants. He went to a bookstore and PhotoRead several books on the subject. As he was leaving, a flash of insight streaked through his mind, drawing him back to the books. He returned to the shelf of books, intuitively grabbed one, and opened the book automatically to the page which offered a clear explanation of the advice.

Needing to learn French, a business woman PhotoRead the English/French dictionary repeatedly for a couple weeks before attending French classes at the Berlitz school in Brussels. Each night after class, she PhotoRead the course manuals and the dictionary. Within three days she had advanced to the second book. School administrators told her she was performing 2-1/2 times better than their previous best student.

A high school defensive football coach repeatedly PhotoRead football play books prior to the start of the season. He discovered during game situations he could predict the opposing team's offensive strategy and respond with the ideal defensive play. His thinking speed and mental alertness was dramatically improved.

A beginning PhotoReader PhotoRead ten books a day for several weeks. He knew the way to master the system was to do it repeatedly so that the process became second nature. One morning he PhotoRead a book on how quantum physics relates to the brain. That afternoon during a slow period of a Minnesota Vikings football game he spontaneously imagined thoughts, ideas, concepts, principles, and theories about physics. Several days later he told colleagues of his experience, one of whom was a physics expert. After quizzing the PhotoReader, the physics expert said that the PhotoReader, as a lay person, knew a heck of a lot about physics. The PhotoReader had tremendous confidence that if he went back to the book and activated it, he would easily gain additional knowledge since PhotoReading had given him a solid basis of understanding.

A university professor PhotoRead her office library. One day, when preparing a major paper, her mind spontaneously activated information she needed. She was sitting back in her office chair facing her bookshelf as she closed her eyes. On the backs of her eyelids she spontaneously imagined six of the books had red dots on them and were connected by red lines. She quickly opened her eyes, looked at the books she had imagined and pulled them from the shelves. As she spread them out she realized her mind had connected the ideal resource information for her paper. Never before had she thought of those six books as having any correlation.

A postal employee entered zip codes into a computer while in the accelerated learning state. He said he became more relaxed and made fewer mistakes than before.

A mystery writer PhotoRead dozens of mystery books to assimilate styles, techniques, dialogs, descriptions, etc. Immediately his writing flowed more easily. He began sending the first or second drafts of chapters to his agent instead of his usual fifth or sixth draft.

The technical director of the virtual reality department of a supercomputer company PhotoRead all the literature he could find on his industry. Since class he had become a prolific writer, presenting professional papers to conferences around the country. He received high professional acclaim by his colleagues.

A electrical engineer at a large power generating utility found himself contributing in a meeting—actually leading the group—on a topic for which he had almost no experience. He was baffled by his obvious expertise. When back in his office he wondered where his sudden influx of knowledge came from. Then he noticed a stack of trade journals on his shelf that he had recently PhotoRead. Sure enough, the most recent journal contained an in-depth analysis of the meeting's topic.

Part Three:

Develop and Integrate Your Skills

8

Tips for Making the PhotoReading Whole Mind System Part of Your Daily Life

Now that you have been exposed to the steps of the system, you can certainly apply them to this book, if you have not done so already. Here are my suggestions on how to proceed.

• Using this book which you know can support you in your current life goals, establish a clear purpose for reading it and enter the ideal state of mind.

• Preview the book for five minutes, noting trigger words as you go.

• PhotoRead the book by following the steps of the procedure in Chapter 5. You can PhotoRead this book in less than three minutes by flipping a page every two seconds. When finished, give yourself the closing affirmations and relax for a few moments.

• Ideally, get up and take a break for a short while. Then come back to activate.

• Activate by mind probing, super reading and dipping. Concentrate on super reading and dipping in the remaining chapters of this book. Take no more than 10 minutes for this. Then, create a one page mind map of the entire book as a great way to summarize all you received by super reading and dipping.

• Pause to review how much information you absorbed during activation. Take a minute to affirm your ability to apply these advanced reading strategies in your daily life. As you do so, you are taking action that could change the way you read forever.

• Finish by rapid reading the last section of this book. I did say that rapid reading starts at the beginning of a book and goes through to the end. I am assuming you have already read it up to here. This is your chance to discover how much faster your reading has become by using the tremendously flexible skills you have learned.

Integrating your skills

You are born with the ability to PhotoRead. However, you are not born with all the skills of the whole mind system fully intact and ready to use. The system is a cluster of learned skills and will take some integration before it becomes second nature to you.

PhotoReading and the other steps in the system are learned just like any other skill—from playing the piano to using a personal computer. If you want to turn a new skill into a habit, learning specialists David W. Johnson from the University of Minnesota and Frank P. Johnson from the University of Maryland have a strategy. I have applied their approach to learning the skills of the PhotoReading whole mind system:

• **Understand why the skills are important and how they will be of value to you.** To learn a skill, you must feel a need for it.

• **Understand the outcome of using the skills and master its component behaviors.** For example, the ability to drive a car results in you safely getting to where you want to go. This larger skill consists of many behaviors, such as starting the car, checking the rear view mirror, signaling turns, steering, accelerating, and applying the brakes.

Often it helps to observe someone who has already mastered the skill perform it several times. Ask that person to describe each component behavior in a step-by-step manner.

• **Find situations in which you can use the skills.** To master a skill, use it again and again. Use the skill for a short time each day until you are sure you have mastered it completely.

• **Ask someone to watch and tell you how well you are performing.** Getting feedback is necessary for staying on course to your goal. In the PhotoReading class we will guide you through PhotoReading five or six books, playing "recognition games," and various activation exercises. These all provide opportunity for direct feedback.

- **Be persistent.** Keep doing it! There is a rhythm to learning most skills: a period of slow learning followed by a period of fast improvement and then a period in which performance remains about the same. These plateaus are quite common in skill learning. If you encounter one, just keep using the skill and remind yourself that another period of rapid improvement is on the way.

- **Load your learning toward success.** As you stretch your capacity, add refinements that you can easily master. For example, gradually increase the number of trigger words you notice while previewing a book for five minutes.

- **Ask friends to encourage you to use the skill.** When you take a PhotoReading class you will have the opportunity to exchange support with other PhotoReaders. The best support network you will ever find for your use of PhotoReading is in the people with whom you attend class.

- **Use the skills until they feel real.** The more you use a skill, the more natural it becomes. While learning a skill, you may feel self-conscious and awkward. It might seem as if you are just going through the motions. That is normal, so do not let this awkwardness stop you from mastering the skill. Do people learn to type by typing only when it feels natural? Of course not. It is through use of the techniques and working through the initial awkwardness that skills are learned.

In summary, it is up to you to apply the techniques presented in this book and apply them in ways that achieve your purposes. If you want to master whole mind reading, then follow these three suggestions: use it, use it, and use it.

Avoid creating an artificial "practice time." This can become drudgery. You have reading you want and need to do. Use the system! You may even consider enrolling in a PhotoReading class. In the meanwhile, dig into those piles of books laying around the house that call you to read them.

Use the PhotoReading whole mind system on all kinds of materials

Whole mind reading can accommodate all printed material.

This includes reports, memos, novels, textbooks, technical manuals, brochures—any documents that you encounter in daily life. As you work with these materials, feel free to adapt the strategies of the system.

When reading a novel, for example, you may want to use some of the steps and de-emphasize others. Some readers enjoy reading a book as much or more than going to the movies. I found out that when my whole mind is engaged, reading a novel is more exciting than a movie.

I prepare as usual by fixing my attention and entering the learning state. Next, I preview the story, looking for the names of significant persons, places, and things. Then PhotoRead the book, which will not spoil the ending.

Then, I follow PhotoReading with rapid reading. Here I might find the activating step (including super reading and dipping) to be less important for my enjoyment of the story.

For larger documents—such as textbooks or technical manuals—a strategy of previewing followed by PhotoReading is the ideal start. Depending on how much of the content you want to recall at a conscious level, use super reading and dipping. Here you might choose not to use rapid reading at all.

Many times, short magazine articles are best previewed, super read and dipped without PhotoReading. Memos and letters are often best handled by previewing followed by rapid reading with high concentration and no regressions.

Used in this way, the PhotoReading whole mind system will significantly reduce the time you spend on routine reading chores. Here are **five instant time management strategies** that will also help:

1. Prioritize your reading. Sort your printed materials into three levels of priority: "A" for matters that are urgent, "B" for items that are important but not urgent, and "C" for items that can be thrown away. Begin using the PhotoReading whole mind system with the "A" priority items.

2. Handle papers only once. Decide how you will respond to each piece of paper the first time you read it. Jot your decision right on letters and memos.

3. Always carry reading materials with you. Use waiting

time for reading. You will be surprised how much you can read in the five or ten minutes between appointments using the whole mind system.

4. Preview everything that is important. If you do nothing else with it, at least preview a document for 30 seconds before filing it.

5. Use the PhotoReading whole mind system at every opportunity. PhotoRead everything you can get your hands on. When the quarterly trade journal arrives or the weekly news magazine is delivered, PhotoRead them. Just take a moment to drop into state and flip the pages before your PhotoFocused eyes. Even if you do not activate, the exposure can serve you in the future.

Study with your whole mind

The PhotoReading whole mind system naturally creates a perfect strategy for moving through a semester of reading. Imagine previewing and PhotoReading every book for the entire semester on the first night after classes. Throughout the night, in your dream state, the material is reviewed and organized according to your needs and purpose.

Every class session you attend becomes a natural activation session. Mind map all your class notes for instant review of the entire lecture. When you get a reading assignment, preview and PhotoRead those chapters. Attend class to activate them, then super read and dip to cover anything else you want to study.

Before tests, PhotoRead your assignments to get yourself in the flow state, then rapid read the sections assigned for the test. Before writing reports, use super reading and dipping to get the core concepts you need, then mind map your first draft.

With these potent study skills, the ease and pleasure of learning will astound you. A PhotoReader, attending a college humanities class had nine books to study during the semester. With one book over 600 pages long, she invested less than 30 minutes reading in order to write a paper that received an "A" grade. She received an "A" for the semester and claimed she had spent less than two hours reading in total.

If you doubt the story, prove it to yourself. Experiment with the following procedure as you study textbooks. The idea here is to study in blocks of 30 minutes, which contain mental preparation and physical breaks. The effect is an increase in concentration, retention and recall of all you study.

1. **Gather all the reading materials you intend to use during this study session.** Lay them out in front of you.

2. **Take three to five minutes to state your purpose and enter the ideal state of mind.** When stating your purpose consider your desired outcome for this study session. Enter the ideal state for learning and repeat affirmations. Phrase your affirmation in the present tense. For example:

- I am ready to absorb chapters 5 and 6 of this physics text to prepare for class tomorrow and answer the questions at the end of the chapter.

- As I study for the next 20 minutes, I do so with full alertness and effortless concentration.

- When I am through studying, I feel refreshed, relaxed, and confident.

- When I call upon this information in the future, I relax and let go. The information flows freely through my mind. I easily retrieve the information I desire.

3. **Begin your study in the flow state of relaxed alertness.** Preview the material for a few minutes, then for the remainder of the 20 minutes use whatever combination of PhotoReading, activating, or rapid reading suits your purpose. Go for zero distractions.

4. **Take a five minute break.** This is essential. Move completely away from your study area, both physically and mentally. Even if you are on a roll and feel as though you could study for hours, take the break! You made a deal with yourself for a specific time commitment. Keep your commitment, because it will build a trust between your conscious and other-than-conscious mind.

5. **Go back to step 2 and repeat the cycle three times for a total of 90 minutes.** Then give yourself a 15 minute break between the 90 minute cycles.

Playing pleasant music softly in the background as you study may add to your relaxation. Studies have found that classical and "new age" music can help make a greater impact on the brain while learning. In the PhotoReading class you receive a Paraliminal Tape titled, *Memory Supercharger*, which helps after studying and before tests. The *Personal Genius* tape is also extremely valuable for learning. You have a certificate for one in this book.

Take tests with your whole mind

When taking tests on materials you have studied using the whole mind system, follow these tips. This will help you remain in a steady state of relaxed alertness throughout the exam:

- **Get into the ideal state of relaxed alertness.**
- **PhotoRead all the questions. Then read the first question.**
- **Answer all the questions that come easily first.** Stay focused on the present moment. Let go of the previous question, as well as any anticipation of the next question.
- **If an answer does not come to you after reading a question, let it go and move to the next question.** The request for an answer to the earlier question has already been given to your other-than-conscious mind. When you have answered all the questions that come easily, go back and re-read those you passed up. The second reading reinforces the request and helps the appropriate answers appear in your conscious mind.
- **Discover how your deeper mind signals you** that it has a correct or appropriate answer to a test question. Rather than over-analyzing the test question, study the signals your other-than-conscious mind is giving you. Pay attention to your intuitive signals. For example, imagine a traffic light which will give you direction. Green means go. Yellow means maybe you know the answer, but you should proceed cautiously. Red means stop, do not answer this one.
- **Release any need you may have to perform well.** The results of any single test fade in importance over time. More often than not, force only leads to frustration. Get what you need by letting go of your need to have it.
- **When taking tests, pause many times to relax more deeply.**
- **During the night before your exam, use audio cassette tapes** that promote relaxation and memory skills. Two of the Paraliminal Tapes I created titled, *Memory Supercharger* and *Personal*

Genius, are excellent for this.

Choose how you will use the
PhotoReading whole mind system

As you finish this chapter, think of a specific reading task that you often face, such as reading reports and trade journals or studying textbooks. Use the whole mind reading system in ways that will accomplish your goal.

Imagine how and when you will use the techniques. For example, you might see yourself previewing the morning paper by scanning the headlines and photo captions. Determine the specific time and place you will use the technique you chose.

The PhotoReading whole mind system is a tool with countless applications. You have just seen yourself experiencing some of them. Now, add another application to your reading repertoire as you learn how to...

9

Share Information Through Group Activation

I hear many business people complain about thick, ugly documents they encounter at work—specification manuals, requests for proposals, stacks of computer printouts, technical manuals for equipment, software manuals, and so on. I see these people's eyes sparkle with anticipation, if not amazement, when I suggest an alternative that involves PhotoReading.

When I first presented PhotoReading at IDS/American Express in Minneapolis, I worked with an information systems and data processing group. After a class session, several participants came up to me. The one holding a stack of reports said, "This course has been very interesting. But how do we use the techniques on *these?*" He dropped the stack on the table with a thud. Feeling a bit threatened, I told him we would cover applications of this sort during the next session.

That afternoon, I cleared my desk and took the first document—a blue covered, computer generated report—and set it in front of me. I read the front cover which said, "CATS Unscheduled Disbursements, Systems External Specifications." My brain instantly overloaded and blew a fuse. My heart started racing at the thought of teaching session five. I could hear the ridicule and feel the humiliation. My palms got sweaty. No doubt about it, I was in document shock.

I numbly opened the front cover and tried to read the table of contents. Nothing made sense. It was all complete gibberish. Now my panic was complete.

Almost instinctively, I stopped everything, took in a deep breath, and dropped into the accelerative learning state. I opened my eyes, entered PhotoFocus, and PhotoRead the report—once right side up, once upside down and backwards. After PhotoReading, I closed my eyes and gave myself the closing affirmation.

Then came the weird part. I opened my eyes and looked at the table of contents again. Miraculously, everything made sense. I went on to preview the report and could clearly see how the entire report was structured, what information was covered, the purpose for it, and the conclusions drawn. I super read and dipped and in minutes I knew exactly what data processing managers needed to know from it. Fantastic!

I bounced through the other documents like a kid in a candy store. It took me between eleven and thirteen minutes to read any one of them—and I understood it well enough to discuss it.

Imagine my confidence at the next session. I described how to read the reports using the PhotoReading whole mind system. One manager commented that I understood the reports better than he— and his department generated similar documents quarterly.

Reading stacks of business or teacher generated papers is simple using the PhotoReading whole mind system. If you need familiarity with a document, prior to a meeting or class, the strategy that follows is a godsend.

Group activation

Say that you manage a group of three people, and that each of these people has differing degrees of expertise about what happens in your company as a whole. One person, for example, often works with the human resource department, another talks frequently to systems analysts in the data processing department, and the third person has responsibilities in marketing and product development.

One day you are handed the software manual for a new company-wide computer system. Looking at the table of contents, you find that you have 600 pages of extra reading to complete in the next week. One option for handling this situation is the traditional one: you and each of your people slog through the manual from start to finish, releasing much hope of sleep for the next few nights.

Instead, try this: hand each of your staff a copy of the manual. Ask each of them to take the manual home for one night, preview it for five to eight minutes, and then spend another few minutes PhotoReading it before they go to sleep. During the next working day meet as a group to activate and discuss the document.

In the meeting, go around the group and ask what they know from previewing the manual. This will insure everyone is starting from a similar frame of reference. Next, give your group an activation assignment. Ask each person to spend a seven to ten minutes super reading and dipping in the manual to find specific information. Give them specific topics to focus on with specific questions related to areas of personal or professional interest.

For example, ask your human resource expert to super read and dip into the manual to judge how this new system will affect the company's need for new personnel or training programs. Ask your system's manager to judge the technical fit with existing systems, and so on.

After completing this assignment, the next step is to activate in a group discussion. Spend five minutes each describing what they learned from super reading and dipping into the text. Let one person create a giant mind map that pools the main points each person describes. Follow the mind mapping with an open discussion, allowing your employees to ask each other questions about the specific points they have made.

Experiment with this strategy, and you will be surprised at the richness and value of the ensuing discussion. As your employees ask and answer questions, they help each other activate the material they have read. In effect, this is PhotoReading followed by group activation.

Watching groups use this strategy, I have seen them reduce reading chores from several hours of wasted time to a matter of a few highly effective minutes. What's more, this process prompts people to share information across specialties—something that is surprisingly rare in the information age. The payoff is concrete: high level people are freed from plowing through manuals for hours at a time; instead, they can return to what they do best. Groups turn into productive decision making forces, using shared information and learning to become even more effective as they go.

This is one of the most powerful tools I know of for coping with information overload and document shock. It is no longer feasible to expect any one person to master all the information on a given topic. Instead, use the PhotoReading whole mind system to create a regular process of sharing information across departments and areas of expertise.

If you wish to use this process in a structured way, the following format describes each step. Use it whenever several people need to share an understanding of a document.

Read entire section

1. Pre-Session Assignment

The beginning of the process includes a memo from the group leader with the reading assignment attached. The memo states the purpose and intended outcome of the meeting.

2. Individual Preparation

Complete the assigned reading in stages:

- Prepare (1-2 minutes).
- Preview the material (3-8 minutes).
- PhotoRead (1-3 minutes).
- Optional: super read and dip (10 minutes maximum).
- Before sleep, visualize activating the materials and successfully accomplishing the group's outcome.

3. Group Activation

Restate the intent of the group. Summarize the reading by describing the document in general terms, discussing the type of report or article, the main point of it, and questions the author is addressing.

Next, assign the sections to be analyzed and the specific kind of analysis you want from each person. For example, one person could look at the report from the position of a management expert. One person could explore what problems are being raised. Another person could examine short range financial implications.

Ask each group member to rapid read the assigned section or super read the entire text for the key ideas they are exploring. Remember to specify the time for completing the task. (Trained PhotoReaders generally activate a 15 to 30 page report in seven to twelve minutes.)

4. Discussion—Analytical Format

Outline the structure and content of the entire document:

• List trigger words. What are their meanings? Do those meanings shift at any point in the text? (Refer back to Chapter 4 on previewing for information on this.)

• List the main propositions. What ideas capture the opinion and facts presented in the document? Arrange these opinions and facts in a logical sequence to discover the key arguments. If you find the conclusion first, then look for the supporting reasons. If you find the reasons first, see where they lead.

• Examine the defined problems and the proposed solutions. What problems does the author solve? Are there any that remain unsolved?

• Critique the text. Discuss the merits and drawbacks of the ideas presented. What arguments do you agree with? What are the points of disagreement?

Discussion—Creative Format

Your group might rather engage in a creative discussion instead of an analytical one. If that is the case, this format will be more appropriate.

• Describe your "feeling response" to the written materials. Keep in mind that feelings set a stage for how information will be interpreted.

• State the facts and information you have received from the text.

• Conduct a brainstorming session about the meaning, relationship, and relevance of this information to the group's outcome.

• Plan what to do about all this information, and establish the group's next step.

The benefits of the PhotoReading whole mind system can ripple throughout your organization and change the way you get things done at work. Shared decision making occurs when everyone shares the same base of information. Using these techniques, individuals keep up with almost no effort or struggle.

A few minutes devoted to previewing and PhotoReading at night is not a major project. Taking ten minutes in a meeting to turn on the whole mind and activate relevant information with a strong purposeful approach to problem solving is enormously productive. When sharing the activated information, the group is totally focused on decision making.

Get your group involved

How do you get your people started today? Buy copies of this book for them. Tell them to preview and PhotoRead the whole book, then activate just this chapter. Do you think that will stimulate their curiosity?

Seriously, it is a good idea that everyone learn these skills. Tell them to use the guide at the beginning called "How to Read This Book," and read the book to level two. This is a one hour investment.

Another way is to bring a certified PhotoReading instructor into your company for a training. Call Learning Strategies Corporation now for information on sponsoring an in-company training.

You can say good-bye to worrying about how to contribute in meetings because you never got to read the report. Gone are the nights of lugging papers home, only to ignore them, and then shamefully let them pile. Now you can stand up and take a powerful lead wherever you are. Information is power for those who know how to access it and share it in useful ways.

Simply do it. The demonstrations of success will happen. You can take specific steps to strengthen your application of these ideas as you learn how to...

10

Enrich Your PhotoReading Experience

The concept of "no pain, no gain" is absurd when it comes to matters of the mind. I heard a comedian say, "My new exercise philosophy is, 'No Pain, No Pain!'" I like that. You simply cannot become more skilled at PhotoReading when beating yourself up.

I enrich my use of the system every time I explore related areas of self development. Discover for yourself that becoming more skilled with elements of PhotoReading actually improves the quality of your entire life in many ways.

Cultivate the eye-mind connection

Extremely fast readers are visual readers. They rely on a direct connection between the eye and the brain. They do not need to subvocalize—that is, mentally hear the words on the page—in order to comprehend written materials. Studies indicate that subvocalizing is not critical to comprehension.

Depend on your eyes alone to deliver the information you want from reading. Many of us have spent years developing a conflicting habit: receiving visual and auditory signals in order to understand our reading. Your brain most likely will not adjust to a total shift overnight. To encourage your development, relax when you read. Do not sweat the comprehension on the first or second pass through material. And praise yourself for doing any and all techniques of the PhotoReading whole mind system.

Consider vision training

Vision Therapy, also known as Functional Vision Training, or Sensory Perceptual Training, may be a way to advance your reading skills. Such training strengthens your eyes and your brain's ability to process written information.

Vision training I received included exercises for converging and diverging the eyes, accommodating my focus from far to near, tracking moving objects smoothly, expanding short term visual memory storage, and enlarging my peripheral vision. Developing these skills results in a stronger, more balanced visual system. The payoff is tremendous efficiency in all visual tasks, especially reading.

Expand your peripheral awareness

Developing peripheral awareness involves looking at your visual field and noticing whatever is not in hard focus. The objective is to pull in information that usually eludes the conscious mind. The benefit is that information in this other 99% of the visual field can be attended to, and responded to, with remarkable efficiency.

Pupil dilation increases peripheral vision. This occurs naturally when light intensity decreases or when the eyes diverge, as in the PhotoFocus state. As an aid to this process, I recommend that you PhotoRead in warmer, softer light.

PhotoReading is designed to open our visual field. Like removing the "flight blinders" of a student pilot, practicing PhotoReading helps you notice more of what is there in front of you—for example, the edges of the book rather than a single word or word phrase.

There are other applications for increased peripheral awareness. With it you increase your responsiveness to visual cues in the environment. The applications become limitless. For example, you can drive more defensively, increase your proficiency in sports such as racquetball and tennis, respond better when playing cards, sing in choirs with greater ease, function in a busy office environment more easily, find items in stores more quickly, and increase your typing speed.

Here are some simple ways to work with peripheral awareness:

Read
Bullets

• When driving the car and looking down the road, notice the sides of the road, pick out movements in the side view mirrors, and read billboards without looking at them.

• Walk with a soft gaze, looking to a point on the horizon, and take in the wide panorama of the world around you.

• When in conversation, notice what items of clothing or jewelry people are wearing while looking only at their face.

• When PhotoReading, pay attention to the edges of the book or the spaces between the paragraphs.

• Work with a martial arts expert. The schools of T'ai Chi and Aikido, which are considered the "softer" forms, are ideal.

• PhotoRead books that teach this kind of awareness. Books on Zen and Meditation are excellent resources. The *Inner Game* books by Tim Galloway describe many of the concepts of Zen Meditation in an application-oriented, Westernized way. These books suggest many exercises that build skills related to PhotoReading.

At first, do not activate these books you PhotoRead. Let your other-than-conscious mind surprise and delight you with increased skills. Notice your experience and discover that magical moments become more commonplace as the quality of your life improves.

Enter states of relaxed alertness

The accelerated learning state occurs when we come in contact with the other-than-conscious processes of the mind. The hallmark of this experience is a state of relaxed alertness.

Enter this state, and notice that you can change the quality of thinking and feeling. In turn, this influences physiology such as the autonomic nervous system, heart rate, pupil dilation, perspiration, and adrenaline secretion. All these functions are controlled at an other-than-conscious level. This means that peaceful thoughts can register directly in the body.

It follows that when you are physically relaxed and mentally alert you have the most flexibility and control over the way you think and feel. Since learning is a process of changing the way you think and feel, learning can take place most easily in this accelerated learning state.

To strengthen your skill at achieving relaxed alertness:

• Establish simple control over diet and exercise. A strong and well nourished body and brain leads to a balanced and healthy

Read
Bullets

mind. Eat low fat, low sugar foods. For PhotoReading, drink lots of water and avoid caffeinated beverages.

• Enroll in a PhotoReading class with an instructor certified by Learning Strategies Corporation. Exchanging information with another person taps into your interpersonal intelligence and often is all that is required to "jump start" your PhotoReading abilities.

• Take a moment now and then to breathe with deep inhalations and slow exhalations. Notice the relaxation and soothing feelings which flow comfortably through your body.

• Mentally count from 50 to 1 while in the accelerated learning state. Simply enter your quiet place (remember page 5-3), then with each breath, count a number or two.

• Listen to Paraliminal Tapes and other relaxing audio programs.

• PhotoRead relevant books on autogenic training, self-hypnosis, guided fantasy, Silva methods, meditation, and contemplative prayer. Remember, you do not have to activate every book in order for the concepts to benefit your life.

• Learn neuro-linguistic programming (NLP). Learning Strategies Corporation offers comprehensive training in NLP for changing behavior. A number of the training sessions help participants access the accelerated learning state.

• Explore meditation. You will discover countless varieties including Yoga and Zen. There are many reputable teachers and centers throughout the world that can teach beginning, intermediate, and advanced courses in meditation. Raja Yoga (meaning "Royal Path of Yoga") is the discipline that led to many of the early discoveries of accelerated learning.

I encourage studying forms of Christian or Eastern meditation. But, please be wary of groups that take choices from you or insist on rigid adherence to practices which deny free will. Those groups may be cults.

Use supportive audio tapes

A proven way to reinforce and enrich whole mind reading skills is with the use of audio cassette tapes. The best tapes affirm your abilities to learn, relax, and establish new behaviors. Use them often.

I developed Paraliminal Tapes which combine progressive relaxation with the technology of NLP. These tapes blend separate tracks of narration. One track is more analytical and "left-brained," guiding you in a step-by-step process to help you accomplish your goal. Another track is more "right-brained," using stories and symbolic imagery to reinforce the tape's central message.

Paraliminal Tapes contain no subliminal messages and are not designed to induce hypnotic trances. Rather, they actually break the negative or self-limiting trances that have kept so many people stuck and unresourceful.

Several of these tapes are specifically designed to support the steps of the whole mind system. They are:

Personal Genius helps you get into the flow state and use the full resources of your inner mind for learning. (Remember, a certificate for a *Personal Genius* tape comes with this book.)

Automatic Pilot helps you get into the flow state and move toward your goals without self-sabotage. This tape is great if you habitually talk yourself out of reading things you want or need.

Get Around To It helps eliminate procrastination and motivates you to take action now. If you find yourself putting off reading, then this tape can really help.

New Behavior Generator helps establish the habit of reading and overcome resistance.

New History Generator helps overcome a history of being a poor reader or of not being good at school.

Anxiety-Free helps overcome anxieties around reading, taking tests, and taking responsibility for your own success.

Belief helps change limiting beliefs which may keep you from enjoying all the benefits of the PhotoReading whole mind system.

Dream Play helps you program and recall your dreams which can be an effective activation tool for PhotoReading.

Prosperity helps you win the benefits of PhotoReading by helping attract a promotion, higher productivity, better grades, etc.

Deep Relaxation helps access the PhotoReading state of relaxed alertness.

Self-Esteem Supercharger helps build a positive self-concept.

These and other Paraliminal Tapes are available from Learning Strategies Corporation at 900 East Wayzata Boulevard, Wayzata, Minnesota 55391. Or feel free to call 800-735-TAPE or 612-475-2250.
Ask for a free catalog.

10-Minute Supercharger helps your mind become mentally alert and physically revitalized. It is great for long study sessions.

Establish outcomes, raise commitment

Having clear, well-formed goals is essential to achieving meaningful results in life. The inner mind is a goal-seeking device and must aim at a specific target in order to hit the mark. To achieve significant benefit from PhotoReading, continually set clear targets. Establish a purpose each time you read. Some suggested ways to support this activity are these:

- **Include a note on your daily "to do" list to use the PhotoReading whole mind system.** Integration of these skills happens as you apply them. Do not worry about practicing them; simply use them whenever you read. The word "practice" implies artificially created time to do something you have to do. Take the pressure off and just add this whole mind approach to handle your everyday reading priorities.
- **Set specific reading goals** and share them with a "PhotoReading buddy" who can review your progress. As you establish goals, set yourself up to win. Rather than pressuring yourself with goals you think you "should" accomplish, set fun goals which represent what you truly want. Set goals which stretch your capabilities; at the same time, set goals you can reasonably accomplish.
- **If you do not get the results you want, go easy on yourself.** Keep playing with options. After all, if you always do what you've always done, you will always get what you've always gotten. Do things differently, confront old habits, and affirm your mind's potential.
- **Have a purpose for everything you read.** You may choose to listen to the Personal Celebration series of audio tapes I developed. You will hear dozens of people, all clients of Learning Strategies Corporation, affirm purpose in who you are, what you do, all you have, and everything you get in your life.
- **Use success teams to get the support you need** in accomplishing your goals. These are groups of three to five PhotoReaders who meet regularly to help each other accomplish their purposes. It is a big commitment to meet every month to

PhotoRead with others, but it has always paid off for those who have done it. For more information on success teams, PhotoRead *Teamworks!* by Barbara Sher and Ann Gottlieb.

Use memory techniques

The "tip of the tongue" phenomenon is an example of knowing something but not being able to consciously articulate it. For many people, this is common with remembering names.

The best technique of letting information bubble up from the other-than-conscious into the conscious mind is to give yourself the space to remember. For example, tell yourself: "I know this person's name. His name is coming to me now." Then, dismiss the issue from your mind and allow your mind to do it.

Consider this rule: *want* it to happen; *expect* it to happen; get out of the way and *let* it happen. This is the essence of a positive attitude towards yourself. It represents a basic trust that your mind is a powerful and capable agency ready to serve you whenever you want. A positive faith in the integrity of your mind is the cornerstone of successful whole mind reading.

Play with your dreams

When you remember your dreams, you build a stronger bridge to your other-than-conscious mind. In turn, this gives you more conscious access to the vast resources of your inner "data bank."

In the PhotoReading class we teach you how to use your dreams to help activate books you have PhotoRead. You can do it too. At first, simply remember your dreams when you awaken. As you do so, you may find yourself having lucid dreams—those in which you consciously respond to the events of your dream. The more frequently you remember dreams, and the clearer and more detailed your dream images, the more likely you are to have lucid dreams.

Motivation is key. For the most part, if you want to remember your dreams, you will. For many people, simply having the intention to remember and reminding themselves of this intention just before bed is enough.

To strengthen this resolve, keep pen and paper beside your bed, and create a mind map of your dreams every time you wake up. This activity helps you remember more dreams in the future.

Another method for remembering dreams is asking yourself each time you wake up: what was I just dreaming? This must be your first thought upon awakening, otherwise you may forget some or all of the dream.

Be patient as you try to remember dreams. When you awaken in the morning, do not move or think of anything else. Pieces and fragments of the dream will come to you. Examine your thoughts and feelings as you lie in bed. This often provides the necessary cues for retrieving the entire dream. Keep at it, even if you recall nothing of your dreams at first.

I developed the *Dream Play* Paraliminal tape to aid in recalling dreams. You can also use this book as a springboard tonight. Much of this book is filled with information that will change the way you look at printed pages forever. This book can help you tap into the powerful reserves of your other-than-conscious mind. Use it as one of the many tools at hand by PhotoReading it before you sleep.

Take the PhotoReading course

Enroll in a PhotoReading course. The four days of the course are different than the book in that you will be assisted by a Learning Strategies Corporation certified PhotoReading instructor. Each instructor has guided the individual successes of many course participants before you. Your individual needs and questions can be addressed as you think of them. More in-depth llustrations and examples are offered that meet your learning style. Plus, there are many experiences during the course which cannot be fully described in book form. They bring rich meaning to the chapters you have read here.

In addition to learning the techniques, you will learn:

- How to PhotoRead and activate your brain to achieve your reading goals with higher comprehension.
- How to reliably enter the accelerated learning state in a matter of moments.
- How to open your perceptual field and see with your mind

what cannot be perceived by your eyes.

- How to instantly balance the hemispheres of your brain with simple physical movement, thereby making reading more effective.

- How to program your mind for new habit acquisition and help break the compulsion to read with inefficient reading techniques.

- How to use your dreams as an activation technique.

- How to make friends with your inner mind, trusting your intuitive guidance to solve problems using the vast data base of your other-than-conscious reserves of mind.

The biggest advantage to attending an intensive course setting is the power of doing something and getting feedback. During the course you will PhotoRead five to six books and play with all of the activation techniques described in this book. We even teach how to PhotoRead a dictionary, think of a word, and know where it is on the actual page.

When you will meet others with like-minded attitudes, you gain the support needed to get you through the learning curve. You may even find some new friends in the process.

Throughout this book I have encouraged you to read other books, enroll in the PhotoReading class, and listen to supportive audio programs such as my Paraliminal Tapes. I do this because, the more information you have, the more accomplished you will be in truly using the innate talents you possess.

Be free to discover what author Peter Kline calls, "the everyday genius" within you. I cannot convince anyone that they possess genius talents. Each person must find this truth within. My sincere wish is that you discover this truth for yourself.

As you strengthen your eye-mind connection, expand peripheral awareness, cultivate powerful mental states, and remember your dreams, you will deepen and expand your skills at PhotoReading. You will experience the culmination of your new skills as you discover syntopic reading in Chapter 11.

A theology graduate school student was referred to PhotoReading by a therapist from his home town. Reading and studying had always been his weaknesses, and school was generally a place of personal turmoil. Although he used PhotoReading faithfully, he was unsure that the system really worked for him. In preparation for his final exam he used the PhotoReading whole mind system to do all the studying he felt necessary. Since it took much less time than he would normally invest, he doubted he was fully prepared. During the exam he was relaxed, confident, and maintained the "flow" state throughout. When he turned in his test he felt anxious, not knowing what to expect, and not feeling all that good about what he had done. His exam came back a few days later covered with praises from his instructor. Comments included, "thorough reading and application," "excellent," "good summary," and "very insightful." The student was at first stunned. Soon his astonishment turned to pleasure. His new found skills were with him to stay.

A thirteen year old boy attended the first PhotoReading course in Mexico. Although he has been sighted in only one eye since birth, he applied the skills of PhotoReading eagerly. A month after the course, one of his teachers asked, "Does PhotoReading really work for you?" His response to her probe was to hand her his dictionary, which he had PhotoRead several times. He told her, "Give me any word and I will tell you where the word is positioned on the page." He correctly identified the position of nine out of ten words, to which the teacher responded, "Hmmm, maybe it does work!"

11

Use Syntopic Reading for Life-Long Exploration

My professor in graduate school told the class to pick a subject in the field of human resource management which we knew nothing about. "Go read all the books you can find on the subject and write a ten to twenty page report on what you learn."

I found twelve books. Using the whole mind system I finished all the books and completed a mind map of my report—all in one afternoon. I typed the report from the mind map and turned it in.

When the paper was returned to me it had only two marks on it: "100%" and "Excellent!" Never before in my undergraduate or graduate work had such a project ever been so easy.

My colleague Patricia Danielson developed the idea into an exercise called, "syntopic reading." She tested it in a follow-up session with PhotoReading graduates in Europe, and it proved wildly successful.

The syntopic reading exercise predominates session four of the PhotoReading course. I describe it late in this book for the same reason we save it for the last day of class. Syntopic reading draws upon all the skills you have developed and takes you to the next level of mastery.

Imagine if you could read three to five books on a subject in just one afternoon. You can with the basic steps of the syntopic reading described in this chapter.

How it works

Let us say you have an interest in a subject and find a book you really want to read. By PhotoReading and activating three additional books on the same subject, you can know the one book better. But here is the best news: it takes less time to apply our system to all four books than it takes to read one using your old reading techniques.

Think of reading as a path of life-long exploration. As we follow this path, we soon discover there are opposing viewpoints about every significant topic. For the skilled reader, differing views create a tension that invites the next level of resolution—a new viewpoint that synthesizes the existing viewpoints. This is an aim of syntopic reading.

People who read well understand many sides of a topic and come to their own conclusions. Syntopic reading ensures that more of your ideas are based on your own thinking. This is done by exposing yourself to various viewpoints and choosing or constructing one that ultimately rings truest for you. Your truth comes from your reasoning, overall knowledge, and reflection on experience—and not just from the last book you read. Often, in fact, you must read several books on the same subject to gain a deeper understanding.

The experience of one PhotoReading student demonstrated how easily she gained the advantages of reading multiple books on a subject. She had returned to school 25 years after high school to get her college degree in a local community college. Prior to taking an essay exam in her history class, she PhotoRead seven books relating to the subject she was studying.

She beamed as she described to me how the words flowed during the exam. She had never felt so relaxed and confident during an essay exam, and she proudly added, "I got an 'A' on the exam!"

She found the natural transition from PhotoReading to syntopic reading—a concept which was actually first described fifty years ago.

Syntopic reading began with Mortimer Adler and Charles Van Doren's classic text *How to Read a Book*. Adler considered the thinking skills used in syntopic reading to be the ultimate goal of a well-read person. We added whole mind reading skills to syntopic reading to help synthesize ideas more efficiently.

One man in a class of mine was in a university doctoral program in education. Writing papers had always been a time-consuming problem for him. He would have to read several books, distill the information, generate his own ideas, and write the paper. After learning syntopic reading, he applied his skills to writing papers at school. He called me several months later. "This is unbelievable!" he exclaimed. "I cannot tell you how easy PhotoReading has made it for me. I can finish, in one afternoon, a paper that used to take me two or three days."

How can it be? It is all in the basic steps of whole mind syntopic reading which follow:

1. Establish a purpose

The first active step of syntopic reading is to state a purpose that has meaning and value for you.

Be clear and specific—it is crucial. Suppose your purpose is to learn money management strategies. Which purpose statement is more effective?

Optional: Read through all 10 steps

- I want to learn more about financial planning, or
- I want to learn effective methods to save money and invest wisely so I can build my financial independence.

The second statement has more kick, because it is clear and specifies a purpose with personal meaning. Meaning also increases long-term retention.

2. Create a bibliography

The second active step is to create a bibliography—a list of books that you plan to read. Preview your books to determine if they fit your purpose. For this exercise, choose non-fiction books by different authors on a subject that you really want to understand.

3. PhotoRead all materials 24 hours before activating

The mind needs incubation time to create new connections. PhotoRead your selected books 24 hours before you plan to activate them. PhotoReading makes the difference in your ability to process ideas at high speeds. During sleep, your brain finds ways to categorize information exposed to it during PhotoReading.

4. *Create a giant mind map*

Have on hand your books, a large sheet of paper, and colored markers for mind mapping. Use mind mapping to take notes during the remaining steps of syntopic reading. In the center of your sheet of paper, write your initial statement of purpose. Leave enough room to revise your purpose statement later if you desire. Also keep in mind that you are not mind mapping the content of any individual book. Instead, you are mind mapping material from all the books that serve your purpose.

Sample syntopic mind map

5. *Find relevant passages*

Super read and dip through each of the books finding passages relevant to your purpose. In this step your purpose reigns supreme over the purposes of the authors. The reason for holding your purpose as the guiding light is to pull out the otherwise obscure passages that can serve your purpose. Continue mind mapping the passages you find.

Let go of your desire to read in too much detail at this point. Use only light dipping throughout the books, and restrict your dipping to relevant passages. You may find during this step that your purpose statement will be refined as the complexities of the topic become clearer.

Think of this as a discussion with the authors of these books. Imagine these authors are sitting around in a circle with you. Ask them a question and let them speak to your purpose. The objective is not to understand their books; it is to understand your purpose.

6. *Summarize in your own words*

If you step back and look at your mind map, you will notice a number of important concepts being addressed. Briefly summarize what you think about the subject so far.

It helps to create a neutral, jargon-free terminology of your own. Different authors may use different words to say the same things. Finding a neutral set of terms creates meaningful associations and makes the concepts your own.

7. Discover themes

Explore your mind map and your books for similarities and differences among the various authors viewpoints. When you reach this stage, you will begin to uncover the central themes that all or most of the authors are attempting to address. Make note of these.

8. Define the issues

When authors have opposing viewpoints, these differences are points of contention or issues. Uncover differing viewpoints, and you will enhance your knowledge about the subject.

In this step you super read and dip to find key points related to these issues. Picture yourself an investigative reporter in a room with your authors. Pose the central questions to each of them.

Go quickly from one book to another, answering one question at a time. As soon as you find it in one book, leave that book and start flipping through the next one.

9. Formulate your own view

As you discover issues and explore various viewpoints, you automatically begin to synthesize your own viewpoint. Look at all sides and take no sides at first. Make a deliberate effort to remain objective and avoid being partial in your analysis.

After gathering enough information, create your own position. Formulate your own opinion based on your research.

10. Apply

Most business people and students have fulfilled their needs by the end of the previous step. That is as far as they want to go with their subject.

When you syntopically read three to five books, you may find one book may be worthy of further study. If you are interested, use the PhotoReading whole mind system to complete your study of that book.

For the person writing a college level paper or detailed

business report, another step is important. After formalizing your position on the subject, you must create an argument to support your view, based on specific information from your books.

Order the key issues in such a way as to throw more light on the subject. Be specific in creating any argument for your position. Always accompany a statement of an author's view with an actual quotation from the text, referenced by the page number.

Create another mind map of your viewpoint before writing a formal report. This saves time and helps you present your ideas clearly.

How much time do you expect to invest in syntopic reading? In the PhotoReading class we give just two forty-five minute periods for activation. That is all. Add that to the steps taken before class to calculate the total commitment.

The investment before class is approximately ten to fifteen minutes per book to select, preview, and PhotoRead. In class we spend ninety minutes in two separate exercises to finish the remaining steps. When finished, most participants recognize that they have achieved 80-90% of what they really want and need.

Most PhotoReaders also discover that any further study of their subject can be accomplished in just one of their books. They can use rapid reading to quickly gather the remaining information they need to feel complete. Depending upon the subject and the book, you might finish this in twenty minutes or four hours.

The cumulative power of syntopic reading

When you look at all the authors listed in the bibliography to this book, you will see the sources of my syntopic reading. Similarly, the PhotoReading course is a product of examining many authors and many researchers. Many authors cited here also referenced many authors—sometimes fifty to one hundred different books and journals.

Every time you syntopically read, you have the accumulated mental energies of hundreds of thinkers with thousands upon thousands of hours of labor and experience backing you in achieving your purpose. When you feel the power of this, you really understand the thrill of syntopic reading. Since you choose the unique combination of authors, you may stumble on a new point of view that has not been considered by anyone.

A stunning example is reported by Patricia Danielson about one of her students. A physician from Brussels used syntopic reading in his field of homeopathy. Every quarter a number of homeopathic physicians from across Europe gather to share research papers. In preparation for a presentation, he syntopically read and mind mapped the major textbooks of homeopathy. When he looked at his mind maps, they seemed nonsensical. He put them in a file for later review.

Two months later, he pulled out his mind maps and laid them on the floor. Amazingly, they all made total sense to him. In fact, the new ideas that came to him were revolutionary. He quickly prepared his paper and a few weeks later presented it at the quarterly meeting.

Doctors at the meeting were astounded with the insights this man had revealed. One doctor commented that never in twenty years had he made the connections explained in this presentation. When the assembly inquired how the PhotoReader had made such leaps in his thinking, he described the PhotoReading process and syntopic reading. The next PhotoReading course in Brussels had seven of those doctors in attendance.

Visualize the process

Take a moment to integrate the ten steps of syntopic reading with a quick visualization. Think of a subject that you would like to study. What purpose do you desire to fulfill? Imagine going to the library and selecting a dozen books on the subject. Briefly look them over to determine which three to five you will take home with you. These are the ones you feel will meet your purpose.

Imagine that evening, previewing and PhotoReading all the books. The next day you awaken raring to go. You create a giant mind map, establishing a clear purpose statement and writing it at the center of the mind map.

Super read and dip to find relevant passages and mind map these. As you notice patterns emerging, add a list of your own terms around the border of your map to summarize your findings. Explore the themes being addressed. Mind map these along with significant points of view which relate to issues of contention between authors. Remember, your objective is not to figure out the books. Your objective is to fulfill your purpose.

Feel the cumulative power of all this information. It is as if the authors were all present, speaking to your purpose. Imagine applying the valuable insights you gain in a most meaningful way for you. As you conclude your visualization, experience the thrill of syntopic reading.

A successful real estate developer was a true self-made man. He dropped out of school in the tenth grade and never looked back. In his entire life of 50 years he had read a mere three books. After learning PhotoReading reported, "It's just wonderful. I've read a dozen books in the last two weeks and I'm loving it. The PhotoReading course has been one of the most enjoyable experiences of my life." One of the biggest changes in his life was his self-esteem as a learner. For many years he never considered himself a person who could learn. Through PhotoReading he demonstrated he could.

Two friends played tennis for years. One of them took the PhotoReading course and PhotoRead five books on tennis. His game immediately improved so significantly that the other man was stunned. When he discovered how the miraculous improvement occurred, he signed up for the next PhotoReading class. The end result was the same improvement in his own tennis game.

An executive went from being computer illiterate ("I mean, I barely even type!") to a daily user of his machine by PhotoReading computer books, magazines and manuals. "After about a month of doing this, I suddenly realized that those stupid machines were starting to make sense!"

12

Questions and Answers for the Beginning PhotoReader

Just knowing the component skills and techniques of the PhotoReading whole mind system is not the end of learning PhotoReading. It is the beginning. Only after you have learned the entire system from this book, can you develop skills in real life. That is when lots of questions may arise.

When you use a technique, you receive feedback. Even if you do not achieve your goal, you will most likely receive indicators of movement in the direction of your goal. Responding to feedback helps you modify your approach and achieve the level of mastery you need.

This chapter explores many of the questions that beginning PhotoReaders ask in their journey to mastery. Return to these ideas occasionally over the next month. As you evolve in your skill development you will gain more and more benefit from the answers.

How can I let go of any limiting beliefs?

Since the ninth grade you have been able to recognize words instantaneously, without having to sound them out. You are already well-versed in the exquisite array of visual patterns that we call the written word. Why do we feel compelled to sound out every word? Learning to read installed a set of training wheels which have never come off. PhotoReading not only removes them, it helps install rockets in their place.

Learning a new skill will confront years of established habitual behavior. You need to go easy on yourself. Learning can be frustrating, especially if you have gremlins.

Gremlins are habits and disempowering beliefs that create negative feelings and stop us from learning. They are worrisome little creatures according to Richard Carson in his book, *Taming Your Gremlin.*

How do you deal with gremlins? If you try to exterminate them, says Carson, they only get bigger. Instead, play with them. Love them to death. More specifically, call to mind the "NOPS" formula: Notice it, Own it, Play with it, Stay with it. With NOPS, any frustration you may feel can be easier to handle and need not become an obstacle to further learning.

"N" Notice your feelings. Feelings are not right or wrong; they just are.

"O" Own your experience. Admit any frustration. Problems we openly acknowledge are solvable; those we deny will only continue.

You can call up many comforting thoughts whenever you feel frustrated with learning. Take a new twist on an old saying: if at first you don't succeed, you are normal. So do it again.

"P" Play with your experience. Push into the tailspin and see what happens. Go deeper into your confusion. Ask yourself questions. Doing so may lead to even greater confusion at first. Be childlike—it is okay to learn.

"S" Stay with it. Too often we interpret frustration as a sign to give up. Instead, see this emotion as an invitation to forge ahead. If you do, you will start producing new results from reading.

With NOPS in mind, learning the PhotoReading whole mind system is a gentle and pleasant experience. It helps us enter the mind set of a child learning to walk. Falling down is not a time for self-castigation or public humiliation. It is a signal to get up, adjust your approach, and try it again. Using the NOPS formula, you can be your own best cheerleader on the journey to mastery.

What is the ideal attitude to maintain while learning the PhotoReading whole mind system?

When it comes to PhotoReading, one of the great traps we face is already knowing how to read. We have certain notions about acceptable speed and levels of comprehension. Then along comes PhotoReading which asks us to change how we approach our reading problems.

Only a completely new paradigm will help see us through the pressures of deadlines and paper blizzards. Sometimes I hear beginning PhotoReaders say, "This is totally redefining what it means to read."

That is okay. In fact, a new definition of reading takes us to a place where we can glimpse new options, the place called "beginner's mind." This concept goes back to the ancient school of Zen Buddhism. Shunryu Suzuki, a Zen master, said, "In the beginner's mind there are many possibilities, but in the expert's there are few." And he added: "We must have a beginner's mind, free from possessing anything, a mind that knows everything is in flowing change. Nothing exists but momentarily in its present form..."

The Japanese turned around their reputation for manufacturing quality products from 1960 to 1980. This turnaround was aided by a cultural mindset that includes the insights of Zen, continuous learning, rigorous quality control, and a willingness to start over completely when old methods no longer serve.

Today we live in a world that requires us to become beginners over and over again in the face of impermanence, continuous change, and chaos. Re-examining what we have been taught about reading is just one example of the need for beginner's mind, and the dizzying pace of change guarantees that we will see more.

You do not have to study Zen or chant mantras to learn PhotoReading. Both the Eastern and the Western approaches to learning contain benefit. There is a place for rules and for being the expert. There is also a place for questioning everything.

PhotoReaders have both attitudes. We honor both the conscious mind and the other-than-conscious mind. The conscious mind sets goals; the other-than-conscious mind finds creative ways to reach them. While keeping our present reading skills, we gain new options.

Using PhotoReading we not only win a new relationship with the printed word, we also find out how to respond when the world changes. As an adult with a beginner's mind, you will rediscover the joy of continual learning.

How long will it take to learn this system?

As an automobile driver, I found learning to pilot an airplane both familiar and strange. A reader learning PhotoReading experiences similarities and radical differences to regular reading. It takes less time to learn the familiar and more time to learn the strange.

There are four stages to learning anything that is different or unusual. The length of time it takes will depend on how you move through the stages of learning. I can illustrate each stage as it applies to learning PhotoReading:

1. In the first stage, you notice piles of unread material and feel a pervasive sense of information anxiety. Even so, you do not recognize the source of this problem, let alone how to respond. Something in your life is broken, but you are not aware of what needs fixing.

At this level it is common to feel fear, sometimes paired with excitement over the possibility of solving the problem. Label this step **Unconscious Incompetence.**

2. Next, you sense that your present reading habits are not serving you well. Those habits, in fact, are a major source of information anxiety. You learn about PhotoReading and even try some of the techniques. These techniques seem unfamiliar. Now you know what is broken, you know what to do, but you are unable to do it yet. Label this stage **Conscious Incompetence.**

3. This third stage represents a quantum leap. You use PhotoReading skills and experience success with them. Even so, these skills are not fully integrated into your life. You still need to remind yourself to use this new approach to written materials. Label this level **Conscious Competence.**

4. Finally, you enter the stage of mastery. Now PhotoReading is so familiar to you that you use it automatically. The techniques become as natural as breathing. You experience not only a new relationship with the printed word, but a new quality of life. You reduce or eliminate those unread piles and continually satisfy your purpose for reading. Label this stage **Excellence.**

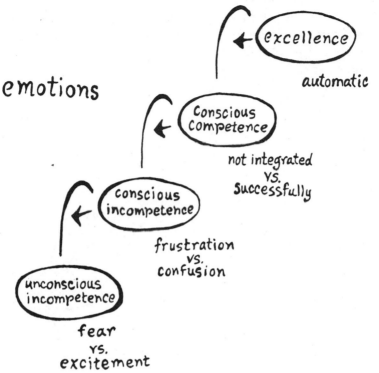

emotions

excellence

automatic

Conscious Competence

not integrated
vs.
successfully

conscious incompetence

frustration
vs.
confusion

unconscious incompetence

fear
vs.
excitement

Learning means passing though the stage of consciously realizing our incompetence—knowing that we do not know something important or that we lack a desired skill. Not surprisingly, certain emotions often accompany this discovery: confusion, frustration, fear, and anxiety.

My suggestion is simple: love it all. No matter what comes up for you as you learn PhotoReading, embrace it. No emotion you experience is wrong, and all your feelings serve a purpose. Confusion can create curiosity. Chaos can lead to clarity.

When I teach PhotoReading classes at Learning Strategies Corporation, I love hearing people move through such feelings. When people say they are confused, I cheer. When they say they are frustrated, I quickly do what I can to move them into confusion. Behind this apparent craziness is a key insight: confusion is one step we climb on the way to excellence. Confusion signals that people are committing an act of learning.

In contrast, approaching problems with a sense of certainty and an unwillingness to let go of old beliefs leads to frustration. We get stuck in a state of learned helplessness, a state of not knowing. These two paths are summarized in the following diagram:

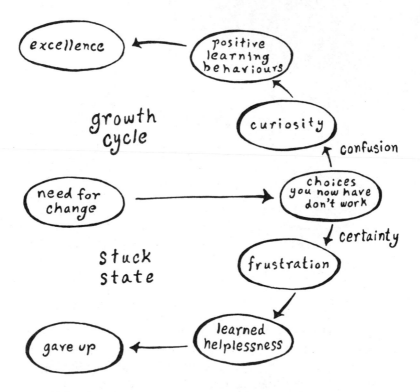

Unfortunately, our educational experiences often lead us down the path of frustration. In the traditional educational model of reading, confusion equals failure, and frustration equals incompetence. The result is that learning stops.

Whatever feelings you experience while learning PhotoReading are fine. Do not suppress any emotional state, any degree of confusion. You may be tempted to compare yourself with others: *I am not doing this right. Everybody else can do this. Why can't I? What is wrong with me?* If you detect such thoughts, let them come to full awareness and be willing to let them go. Remind yourself that conscious competence is coming your way.

Reading gets right to the heart of self-image. Our self-concept is often bound up with our success as learners, and much of our experience with learning ties to reading. I find that people label themselves as poor readers too readily and thus feel ineffective. Such frustration quickly tarnishes our self-image.

The alternative is to accept the emotional ups and downs of learning, to see them as a natural and graceful dance. If you do, you will shorten the path to excellence.

What state of mind should I be in when using the PhotoReading whole mind system?

Think about times when you have been absolutely absorbed in reading. It is important for us to explore those experiences in more depth, because, at those moments, you are transformed into a skilled, powerful reader—effortlessly.

Remember what those times were like. Perhaps you were engrossed in a novel. Maybe you were savoring a love letter. Or perhaps you were solving a murder mystery. In any case, a curious thing happens: you are unaware of anything else going on around you. It is as if the pictures, images, and feelings inside you are more important than the book in front of you. You are no longer reading words—you have stepped into another reality. What is going on behind your eyes is far more important than what appears in front of them.

People describe these experiences with remarkably similar language. "I lost all track of time and place." "I was not conscious of words on a page." "I was just seeing movies in my mind." "I absorbed the words without effort." "Words just flowed from the page to my mind."

Flow—that is a handy word for it. It captures the key features of the experience: ease, fluidity, lack of effort, absorption, concentration, softness, relaxation, efficiency, and enhanced productivity.

Although this experience sounds like an altered state of consciousness, there is nothing abnormal about it. Human beings have known about the "flow experience" for hundreds of years, using a variety of terms to describe it. The *Tao te Ching*, a spiritual text from China by Lao Tsu, speaks of effortless action, or non-action. Psychologist Abraham Maslow spoke of "peak experiences," describing them in a similar way. A popular book from the 1970s, *The Inner Game of Tennis*, explained how athletes could cultivate flow states. It was followed by similar books for other sports.

> Stephen Mitchell, a translator of the Tao, describes the flow state: A good athlete can enter a state of body-awareness in which the right stroke or the right movement happens by itself, effortlessly, without any interference of the conscious will. This is a paradigm for non-action: the purest and most effective form of action. The game plays the game; the poem writes the poem; we can't tell the dancer from the dance.

Recently, Mihaly Csikszentmihalyi, a psychologist from the University of Chicago, revealed that flow experiences can happen to anyone. His studies of this state have included clerks, assembly-line workers, athletes, engineers, and managers. He says flow states bear a strong resemblance to other well-known phenomena—hypnosis and meditation.

Ah, but if we could only flip a switch and enter that flow state whenever we read. We would be in states of deep attention, free of effort or strain, working smoothly, quickly, and efficiently. We would be relaxed, active, and alert, all at the same time. Reading would be a breeze—as easy to flow through technical information as a novel.

The PhotoReading whole mind system is that switch. The flow state is your birthright, one of your potentials as a human being. Through PhotoReading, you get a chance to choose this experience instead of leaving it to chance. This state is not a fluke or some kind of out-of-body experience. Rather, it is a naturally occurring event, and the secret is to make it habitual during all your reading.

What do accelerated learning and PhotoReading have in common?

As a child, you naturally used strategies of accelerated learning to accomplish the monumental tasks of learning to walk and talk. Nothing we learn as adults will equal the complexity of those tasks.

The skills of accelerated learning are still with us from childhood, obscured as they might be from years of abuse, misuse, and disuse. We simply need to reawaken our mastery and apply it to the task of reading. The PhotoReading whole mind system draws heavily from accelerated learning, making it easy and fun to learn and use.

One of the best known researchers in the study of accelerated learning is Georgi Lozanov, a Bulgarian psychologist. Dr. Lozanov has written many papers supporting the claim that we use barely ten percent of our brain capacity. He and his staff of researchers believe that we can systematically learn to tap the hidden reserves— the other ninety percent—of the mind. He developed his findings into an applied system for learning.

Lozanov's methods allow both hemispheres of the brain to work together as an orchestrated team. When that happens, our capacity to learn increases exponentially.

Lozanov claimed you can expose yourself to vast amounts of information, absorb it effortlessly, and use it when you need it. Those are precisely the skills we need to survive in the age of information overload and document shock.

At the heart of Lozanov's learning methods are three steps: decoding, concert, and activation which parallel the PhotoReading whole mind system. Decoding is a "once over lightly"—a quick overview of the material to be learned.

During the concert session, learners enter a state of relaxed alertness to receive a more complete exposure to the material. This information is often presented as a story or play and accompanied by classical music playing in the background.

Finally, learners activate the material, that is, call it to the conscious mind and apply it. Instead of drill sessions and rote memorization, activation uses group discussion, games, skits, and other non-traditional methods.

See the connection? Lozanov's decode-concert-activate is our preview-PhotoRead-activate. The PhotoReading whole mind system incorporates many aspects of Lozanov's methods as does the teaching of the PhotoReading course.

I know I rely too heavily on my conscious rational mind. What else can I do?

In the early 1980s, Howard Gardner, a Harvard psychologist, developed a body of ideas that perfectly complements Lozanov's. Gardner said that our schooling works mostly on two kinds of

Read Bullets

intelligence: those that involve language and logic. Gardner concluded that this was only a small part of the picture, however. A more accurate view of intelligence includes all of the following capacities:

- Linguistic Intelligence—the ability to skillfully describe the world with words.
- Logical-Mathematical Intelligence—the ability to represent the world with numeric symbols and manipulate those symbols according to the rules of logic.
- Musical Intelligence—the ability to appreciate and use the non-verbal "language" of melody, rhythm, harmony, and tone color.
- Spatial Intelligence—the ability to perceive the visual world accurately and recreate it in the mind or on paper.
- Bodily-Kinesthetic Intelligence—the ability to use the body for skilled self-expression or as a tool for learning.
- Interpersonal Intelligence—the ability to perceive and understand other people's feelings and desires.
- Intrapersonal Intelligence—the ability to clarify personal values and gain insight through solitude.

Think of a time you learned something masterfully. Consider which of the seven intelligences you used. You already know how to excel at learning and can do so again at any time. Use the strengths you already possess.

Imagine applying all seven intelligences plus intuition to your reading. The PhotoReading whole mind system helps you do exactly that. All your intelligences are invited to the act of reading. In this sense, PhotoReading is not a reading program but a learning program—a set of strategies for learning anything. Anything.

How does activation tap into the other-than-conscious mind?

According to Dr. Win Wenger, author of *A Method for Personal Growth and Development*, the storage capacity of the inner mind exceeds the capacity of the conscious mind by ten billion to one. These are the reserves of the mind which we draw from during activation.

An example of activation is the tip of the tongue phenomenon that often takes place in remembering names. You know the scene: you see a familiar person at a party, but his or her name slips your mind. You try for a minute to recall the name. This stimulates the neural circuitry of your brain. Then, a few minutes later, the name suddenly flashes in your mind, often while you are talking to someone else and not consciously trying to remember it. Your brain generated the name based on the stimulation of neural pathways established when you first learned the person's name.

Activation can also take place on a grander scale. A writer I know practices meditation which is another way of entering the state of relaxed alertness we cultivate in PhotoReading. He says that some of his best ideas come during periods of meditation, particularly when he is struggling with the content or structure of a manuscript. Frequently, outlines for entire books come to him in this way.

Artists of all types describe similar events in their lives. Aaron Copland, the distinguished American composer, said that writing music begins with transcribing themes that blossom spontaneously from within. As he put it:

> The composer starts with his theme; and the theme is a gift from Heaven. He doesn't know where it comes from—has no control over it. It comes almost like automatic writing. That is why he keeps a book very often and writes themes down whenever they come.

We do not have to be great composers or writers to draw on these deep, creative reserves. We need a relaxed alertness along with a gentle request for the ideas we seek to surface in the conscious mind.

This has profound implications. The secret is just to get out of the way and let ourselves PhotoRead.

Will trying harder help me learn this?

PhotoReading may seem like a bundle of paradoxes, because it is. Think about what I am suggesting: to get more out of your reading, spend less time with it; to gain more information, do not worry about conscious comprehension; to succeed (at reading), quit trying so hard and start playing; and to get what you want, let go of your need for results.

During one course I met a woman who understood this perfectly. Soon after we began PhotoReading books, her percentages of correct answers on comprehension tests climbed into the 90s and stayed there. I asked her how that happened. "I simply decided up front that I have nothing to prove. If the techniques work, fine. If they don't, fine. For me the important thing is to simply experience a new approach to reading."

Wherever I teach PhotoReading, I find the same attitudes in successful PhotoReaders. People who "try hard to do really well" with PhotoReading often strap themselves with a big responsibility. Right away, they feel a personal obligation to prove or disprove the whole mind reading system. That is like wanting to take the final exam in calculus before you have learned how to add—and then claiming that you are lousy in math.

You do not have to believe everything about PhotoReading up front. A little skepticism about the technique is fine. No amount of testimonials can replace the results you produce with your own efforts. Be willing to give PhotoReading a fair trial and remain open for pleasant surprises. A requirement for success is an open mind.

I urge people to ease into the experience of PhotoReading— to play, embrace confusion, and tame the gremlins. Ironically, it is when we stop trying so hard to succeed that our intuition flowers and we rekindle our natural skill at learning. When we let go of success or failure, we start to get what we want.

When will I attain the levels of comprehension I need?

Remember that the PhotoReading whole mind system is based on multiple passes through printed material. First we preview. That can be followed, as we choose, by PhotoReading, super reading, dipping, and rapid reading.

Comprehension comes in layers. Previewing gives us a sense of structure. By using the remaining steps of the system, we build on that foundation, gaining a level of comprehension that is consistent with our purpose. This approach frees us.

> Notice it.
> Own it.
> Play with it.
> Stay with it.

Perhaps this feels like full comprehension is delayed—that you are not getting the "goodies" from your reading as soon as you want them. My suggestion is to greet this feeling with the NOPS formula and discover what emerges.

For example, a PhotoReader took a course during his doctoral program in which he had to read 20,000 pages. Most students in that program take between six and nine months to finish the required reading and write the necessary papers. For an entire week he previewed and PhotoRead. The next week he found nothing came to him as he tried to activate the books and write his papers. He expected to know the material. In frustration, he let it all go, feeling he had wasted the week.

The following week the PhotoReader entered the *beginner's mind*. He activated the books, astonished that everything made sense to him. His writing flowed, and he finished the course, receiving an "A" for his work. His total investment was only three weeks from the time he started.

Was the second week of activation a waste? Or was it the essential period of incubation and fine tuning necessary to achieve the end result?

A PhotoReading student described his experience like this:

"I realized that when using the whole mind reading system, I am actually adding time to do extra things to my reading. I naturally resisted. I could just start reading and comprehending as I go. Or, I could use this new system—adding time to preview and PhotoRead before I could activate for comprehension. My natural response was, why? Why not just get into it?

"I've been telling my kids for years that you have to invest a little bit extra in the learning curve up front before the payoff comes. When you go to school, it is not the information you need. What you are really learning is how to learn—so when you get into the real world, you will be able to get where you want to go in life. Here, I had been giving this advice without taking it myself!

"I soon discovered that the few minutes I invested up front paid back huge dividends. I could save hours reading reports by taking five minutes to preview and PhotoRead. I could save ten to eighteen hours or more on books that used to take twenty hours to read in my old ways."

Read Bullets

In summary this chapter helped you learn:

• The NOPS formula—notice it, own it, play with it, stay with it—will help overcome frustrating habits which prevent learning.

• The beginner's mind is the perfect mindset to maintain during the PhotoReading whole mind system.

• There are four levels you must progress through when learning a new skill.

• Confusion is an appropriate experience during any learning activity.

• The PhotoReading whole mind system uses flow states of consciousness.

• Dr. Lozanov's accelerated learning is a model for the PhotoReading whole mind system.

• We use all seven intelligences described by Dr. Gardner with the PhotoReading whole mind system to make your reading multi-dimensional and more useful.

• The other-than-conscious data base we access while PhotoReading outweighs the data base of the conscious mind by ten billion to one.

• The goal of comprehension is achieved in layers. Paradoxical as it may seem, to achieve your goal, you must let it go.

The PhotoReading whole mind system works. You must use it to demonstrate the benefits in your own life. For this, you need to understand just one more secret...

13

The Secret of the PhotoReading Whole Mind System

The true secret of PhotoReading at 25,000 words per minute is that you already have the ability. Your brain is hardwired for genius. Rediscover your natural genius, play with it, and allow it to become part of your everyday life.

Actively encourage yourself. You will discover that you have abilities reaching far beyond PhotoReading.

A call to active reading

I am privileged to have studied the most masterful learners in the world—babies. Babies are active, purposeful, goal oriented, insatiable learners. For twelve years, my wife and I have watched our three children engage the physical and mental universe. Their hunger to make sense of life is enormous.

Although our three boys are now well beyond the baby stage, they still actively explore their world. Learning is active; activity is the fuel of genius. Our genius fades when passivity takes over.

Television teaches us to be passive. It tells us to just wait, everything we want will come to us—right after this commercial. If reading becomes passive, our genius is stifled.

Regardless of what type of reading you do, stay active. The more active you are, the more fluent your reading becomes and the more effective you will be at achieving the results you desire. Fluent readers maintain a high degree of focus by reading purposefully and by asking questions of the author as they read. Concentration, the essence of active reading, is not nearly so much a discipline as it is an attitude.

Realize that you are reading by choice and that you want to create value for yourself. Choice makes a real difference in how easily you accomplish your purpose for reading, be it a desire to gain information and skills, to evaluate ideas, or to simply relax. When you consciously choose to read, you engage your mind's full capability.

As I write these words, I think of Georgi Lozanov, the grandfather of accelerated learning. Early in his career, Lozanov believed the purpose of his methods was to eliminate fear from the classroom and increase people's suggestibility—their ability to receive information on an other-than-conscious level. Over the years, his thinking changed, and his overriding goal became to offer learners more choices.

This is precisely the aim I have for you in reading. My goal in this book has been to lay out a new paradigm for reading and an accompanying set of tools that maximize your choices when interacting with the printed page.

Make the PhotoReading whole mind system your ally as you become a more active, purposeful, and demanding reader. Read with speed and efficiency. Take the opportunity to extend your understanding beyond your current limits. Above all, use your mind's full potential to accomplish your personal and professional goals, and discover an abiding joy in the process. You can do it!

A new scenario, a closing thought

Remember the scenario of choice from Chapter 2? Let us return to it for a moment. You are ready to enjoy any part of it you desire.

You begin each work day knowing that you have the information needed to make effective and timely decisions. Those old stacks of unread mail, memos, reports, newsletters, manuals, and journals have vanished. Reading technical reports, a task that used to consume hours of your time, now requires only about 15 minutes per document. Your desk is clear. You are all caught up.

This quality extends to your home life as well. You live a largely clutter-free life. Gone are the piles of untouched books, magazines, newspapers, and mail that once crowded your living space. You keep up with the latest daily news in 10-15 minutes a day. Now you consistently find time for novels, magazines, and pleasure reading that go beyond the immediate demands of your job.

Your advanced reading abilities have also erased old fears about further education and training. You take courses to complete degrees, gain promotions, learn new skills, expand your knowledge, and satisfy your general curiosity. You glance at course outlines knowing that you can stay ahead of the required reading and perform with excellence. Often you can complete the reading for an entire semester of a college course during the week you purchase the textbooks. Class reading assignments during the semester feel like review of what you already know. The background reading of a half-dozen books for required papers takes only an hour or two.

Your whole experience of reading has changed. Whenever you read, you do so with a sense of effortlessness and relaxation. The core concepts and key details of what you read are readily available to you. You have become more articulate in conversation, more fluent and persuasive in your writing. You find it easier to win approval for your proposals, because your recommendations are backed by solid evidence. Other people comment on the breadth of your reading and depth of your subject knowledge.

What is more, you finish your reading tasks with time to spare. You can absorb several books in the time it formerly took you to read one. You can extract what you want from entire magazines in the time you used to read one article. In a single sitting, you pare down or eliminate your "to be read" piles. And with the extra time, you consistently complete the top-priority tasks on your to-do lists. In the process, you free up time to goof off as well.

As you embrace the possibilities, savor the experience. What is your commitment now? What step can you take in the next 24 hours to make more of this scenario a reality for you?

Peter Singe, in his book *The Fifth Discipline*, offers a perfect summary:

> The learning process of the young child provides a beautiful metaphor for the learning challenge faced by us all: to continually expand our awareness and understanding, to see more and more of the interdependencies between actions and our reality, to see more and more of our connectedness to the

world around us.

We will probably never perceive fully the multiple ways we influence our reality. But simply being open to the possibility is enough to free our thinking.

Change is as inevitable in our lives as it is in the world around us. PhotoReading, a catalyst for personal growth, frees our thinking and expands our awareness to cope effectively with change. With the skills of the PhotoReading whole mind system, PhotoReaders adjust to the changes in their schools, workplaces, professions, societies, nations, global community, and planet.

With PhotoReading, you can actively pursue mastery in the face of change—by choice. Choose now to master any part or all of the PhotoReading whole mind system. Every action you take leads to your personal excellence.

Quick Reference Guide:

The Steps of the PhotoReading Whole Mind System

One of the maxims of this book is to forget about "practicing" with the PhotoReading whole mind system. Instead, just use it.

To reinforce what you have learned from PhotoReading, choose another book you want to read and apply each of the steps listed below. The sooner you do this, the better. Either do it now, or set a time now to do it in the next three days.

Use this guide whenever you need to as a refresher.

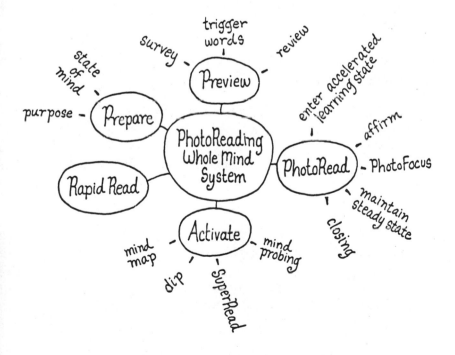

Step 1: Prepare
Clearly state your purpose for reading.

(22)

Enter the ideal state of mind for learning. This is the state of relaxed alertness.

(23)

Step 2: Preview
Survey the written materials.

(24)

Pull out trigger words from these materials.

(25)

Review the information you have uncovered and establish your goal for going further.

(26)

Step 3: PhotoRead
Prepare to PhotoRead.

(27)

Enter the accelerative learning state.

(28)

Affirm your personal abilities and the goal you will achieve from these materials.

(29)

Enter the PhotoFocus state by getting a fixed point of awareness (tangerine technique) and the "blip page."

(30)

Maintain a steady state while turning pages and chanting. Keep your breathing deep and even.

(31)

In closing, affirm the impact the information has had and your ability to activate it.

(32)

Step 4: Activate
Ideally, wait a few minutes, or overnight, after previewing and PhotoReading before activating. This is a period of incubation.

(33)

Probe your mind. Ask yourself questions about the material you PhotoRead. This starts your activation.

(34)

Super read the parts that attract you. Move your eyes quickly down the center of the page to trigger large blocks of text into conscious awareness.

Dip into the text to read selected passages and answer specific questions you asked yourself.

The ideal state of mind for activation is one in which you are attentive to subtle cues in the periphery of your awareness.

 Create a mind map by making a visual diagram of the key ideas from the written materials.

Explore other forms of activation including discussions and dreaming that use multiple intelligences.

Step 5: Rapid Read
Move rapidly through the text, reading comfortably from start to finish without stopping. Take as much time as you desire. Vary your reading speed depending on the complexity and importance of the material.

 Syntopic Reading
1. Establish a purpose.
The first active step of whole mind syntopic reading is to state a purpose that has meaning and value for you.
2. Create a bibliography.
The second active step is to create a bibliography—a list of books that you plan to read. Preview your books to determine if they fit your purpose.
3. PhotoRead all materials 24 hours before activating them.
The mind needs incubation time to create new connections. PhotoRead your selected books 24 hours before you plan to activate them.
4. Create a giant mind map.
Keep your books, a large sheet of paper, and some colored markers on hand for mind mapping. Use mind mapping to take notes during the remaining steps of syntopic reading.

5. Find relevant passages.

Super read and dip through each of the books to find passages that are relevant to your purpose.

6. Summarize in your own words.

Step back and look at all the passages you have written on your mind map. Briefly summarize what you think the subject is all about using your own terminology.

7. Discover themes.

Look for similarities and differences between author's points of view. What are the predominant themes that all the authors seem to address. Make note of these.

8. Define the issues.

Opposing viewpoints between authors are the key issues about your subject. Understanding these points of contention greatly enhances your knowledge on the subject. Super read and dip to find key points related to these issues.

9. Formulate your own view.

In discovering issues, you begin to synthesize your own viewpoint. The skilled syntopic reader looks at all sides and takes no sides at first. After gathering enough information, formulate your own position.

10. Apply.

According to your own needs, apply the knowledge you have acquired.

PhotoReading™

Bibliography

Adler, Mortimer J., & Van Doren, Charles. *How to Read A Book*. New York: Simon & Schuster, 1972.

Bennet, J. Michael. *Efficient Reading for Managers*. AMA Extension Institute, 1981.

Barker, J. *Future Edge: Discovering the New Paradigms of Success*. New York: William Morrow & Company, Inc., 1992.

Berg, H. *Super Reading Secrets*. New York: Warner Books, Inc., 1992.

Bieda, Margaret R., & Woodward, Vinola S. *Realizing Reading Potential*. Chicago: Holt, Rinehart and Winston Inc., 1971.

Bruner, J. *The Process of Education*. Cambridge: Harvard University Press, 1961.

Buzan, T. *Make the Most of Your Mind*. New York: Simon & Schuster, 1984.

Buzan, T. *Use Both Sides of Your Brain*. New York: E.P. Dutton, 1976.

Carson, R. *Taming Your Gremlin*. New York: Harper Perennial, 1983.

Caskey, O., & Flake, M. *Suggestive-Accelerative Learning: Adaptions of the Lozanov Method*. Texas Tech. University, 1976.

Caskey, O. L. *Suggestive-Accelerative Learning and Teaching*. Englewood Cliffs, NJ: Educational Technology Publications, 1980.

Cheek, Earl H. Jr., & Collins, Martha D. *Strategies for Reading Success*. Columbus: Charles E. Merrill Publishing Company, 1985.

Clark, B. *Optimizing Learning: The Integrative Education Model in the Classroom*. Columbus: Merril, 1986.

Cohen, Elaine Landau, & Poppino, Mary A. *Reading Faster for Ideas*. Chicago: Holt, Rinehart and Winston Inc., 1984 .

Covey, S. *The Seven Habits of Highly Effective People: Restoring the Character Ethic*. New York: Simon & Schuster, 1989.

Csikszentmihalyi, M. *Flow: The Psychology of Optimal Experience*. New York: Harper & Row Publishers, 1990.

Cudney, M. & Hardy, R. *Self-Defeating Behaviors: Free Yourself from the Habits, Compulsions, Feelings, and Attitudes That Hold You Back*. New York: HarperCollins Publishers, 1991.

Diamond, Marian Cleves. *Enriching Heredity*. New York: The Free Press, 1988.

Dixon, N.F. *Preconscious Processing*. Chichester, NY: Wiley, 1981.

Dixon, N.F. *Subliminal Perception: The Nature of a Controversy.* New York: McGraw-Hill, 1971.

Doman, Glenn. *How to Teach Your Baby to Read.* Garden City, NY: Dolphin Books, 1975.

Donovan, R. & Woner, J. *Whole-Brain Thinking.* New York: Morrow, 1984.

Dudley, Geoffrey A. *Rapid Reading.* Northamptonshire: Thorsoms Publishers, Ltd., 1977.

Edwards, Betty. *Drawing on the Right Side of the Brain.* Los Angeles, California: J. P. Tarcher, 1979.

Ellis, D. *Becoming a Master Student.* Rapid City, SD: College Survival, Inc., 1985.

Fader, Daniel N. & McNeil, Elton B. *Hooked on Books: Program & Proof.* New York: Berkley Medallion Book, 1968.

Ferguson, M. "Dyslexia could be caused by roving 'orientation point.'" Brain/Mind Bulletin, Vol. 9, No. 14. 1984.

Finkel, R. *The Brain Booster.* Englewood Cliffs, NJ: Prentice-Hall, 1983.

Fisher, Dennis F., & Peters, Charles W. *Comprehension and the Competent Reader, Inter-Specialty Perspectives.* New York: Praeger Publishers, 1981.

Flesh, Rudolf. *Why Johnny Still Can't Read.* New York: Harper Colophon Books, 1981.

Funk, Dr. Wilfred & Lewis, Norman. *30 Days to a More Powerful Vocabulary.* New York: Washington Square Press, Inc., 1942.

Gardner, Howard. *Frames of Mind: The Theory of Multiple Intelligences.* New York: Basic Books, 1983.

Glasser, William. *Schools Without Failure.* New York: Harper & Row, 1969.

Hampden-Turner, C. *Maps of the Mind.* Chicago: Macmillan, 1981.

Jensen, E. *Super Teaching: Master Strategies for Building Student Success.* Del Mar, CA: Turning Point for Teachers, 1988.

Jewell, Margaret G., & Zintz, Miles V. *Learning to Read Naturally.* Dubuque, Iowa: Kendall/Hunt Publishing Co., 1986.

Kline, Peter. *The Everyday Genius: Restoring Children's Natural Joy of Learning.* Arlington, VA: Great Ocean Publishers, 1988.

Kump, Peter. *Breakthrough Rapid Reading.* West Nyack: Parker Publishing Co., Inc., 1979.

LaBerge, S. *Lucid Dreaming.* Los Angeles, CA: J.P. Tarcher, 1985.

LaBerge, S. & Rheingold, H. *Exploring the World of Lucid Dreaming.* New York: Ballantine Books, 1990.

Lakein, A. *How To Get Control of Your Time and Your Life.* New York: Signet, 1973.

Leahey, T. A., & Harris, R. J. *Human Learning.* Englewood Cliffs, NJ: Prentice-Hall, 1985.

Learning Strategies, edited by O'Neil, H.F. New York: Academic Press, 1978.

Lorayne, Harry & Lucas, Jerry. *The Memory Book.* New York: Ballantine Books, 1975.

Lozanov, G. *Suggestology and Outlines of Suggestopedy.* New York: Gordon and Breach, 1978.

Bibliography

Lozanov, G. *Suggestion in Psychology and Education*. New York: Gordon and Breach, 1978.

Mares, Colin. *Rapid and Efficient Reading*. New York: Emerson Books, Inc., 1967.

McCarthy, M. *Mastering the Information Age*. Los Angeles, CA: J.P. Tarcher, 1991.

Morehouse, L., & Gross, L. *Maximum Performance*. New York: Simon & Schuster, 1977.

National Academy of Education. *Becoming a Nation of Readers: The Report of the Commission on Reading*. Washington, D.C.: U.S. Department of Education, 1984.

Novak, J. D., & Gowin, D. B. *Learning How to Learn*. New York: Cambridge University Press, 1984.

Ostrander, S., & Schroeder, L. *SuperLearning*. New York: Delacorte Press, 1979.

Pauk, Walter, & Wilson, Josephine. *Reading for Facts*. New York: David McKay Co., Inc., 1974.

Perfetti, Charles A. *Reading Ability*. New York: Oxford University Press, 1985.

Peterson, Lloyd R. *Learning*. Glenview, IL: Scott, Foresman and Company, 1975.

Prichard, A., & Taylor, J. *Accelerating Learning: The Use of Suggestion in the Classroom*. Novato, CA: Academic Therapy Publications, 1980.

Raygor, Alton L., *Reading for the Main Idea, 2nd Ed.* New York: McGraw-Hill Book Co. 1979.

Raygor, Alton L. & Wark, David M. *Systems for Study*. New York: McGraw-Hill Book Company, 1970.

Reese, M., Reese, E., Van Nagel, C., & Siudzinski, R. *Megateaching and Learning: Neuro-Linguistic Programming Applied to Education*. Southern Institute Press, Inc. 1985.

Richardson, Glenn E. *Education Imagery*. Charles C. Thomas Publishing Co., 1983.

Rico, Gabrielle L.*Writing the Natural Way: Using Right-Brain Techniques to Release Your Experience Powers*. Los Angeles: J. P. Tarcher, 1983.

Rosenthal, Robert & Jacobson, Lenore. *Pygmalion in the Classroom*. New York: Holt, Rinehart and Winston, 1968.

Rubin, Dorothy. *Reading and Learning Power, 2nd Ed.* New York: Macmillan Publishing Co., 1985.

Schaill, William S. *Seven Days to Faster Reading*. No. Hollywood, Ca.: Wilshire Book Company, 1976.

Schuster, D. H., Bordon, R. B., & Gritton, C. E. *Suggestion-Accelerative Learning and Teaching: A Manual of Classroom Procedures Based on the Lozanov Method*. Ames, IA: Box 1316, Welch Station, ED-136566.

Schuster, D. H., & Gritton, C. *Suggestive Accelerative Learning Techniques*. New York: Gordon and Breach Science Publishers, 1986.

Senge, P. *The Fifth Discipline*. New York: Doubleday, 1990.

Sher, B. *Teamworks!* New York: Warner Books, 1989.

Sherbourne, Julia Florence. *Toward Reading Comprehension, 2nd Ed.* Lexington, Massachysetts: D.C. Heath and Co., 1977.

Slavin, Robert E. *Cooperative Learning*. Washington, D. C.: National Education Association, 1982.

Smith, Frank. *Reading Without Nonsense.* Columbia University, New York: Teachers College Press, 1979.

Smith, Frank. *Writing and the Writer.* New York: Holt, Rinehart and Winston, 1982.

Sparks, J.E., & Johnson, Carl E. *Reading for Power and Flexibility.* Beverly Hills: Glencoe Press, 1970.

Stauffer, Russell. *Teaching Reading as a Thinking Process.* New York: Harper & Row, 1969.

Suzuki, S. *Zen Mind, Beginner's Mind.* New York: John Weatherhill, Inc., 1970.

Twing, James E. *Reading and Thinking: A Process Approach.* Chicago, Illinois: Holt, Rinehart and Winston, Inc., 1985.

Verny, Thomas. *The Secret Life of the Unborn Child.* New York: Summit, 1981.

Vygotsky, Lev. *Thought and Language.* Cambridge: MIT Press, 1962.

Wainwright, Gordon R. *How to Read for Speed and Comprehension.* Englewood Cliffs, NJ: Prentice Hall, Inc., 1977.

Walcutt, Charles Child, Lamport, Joan & McCracken, Glenn. *Teaching Reading.* New York: Macmillan Publishing Co., Inc., 1974.

Waldman, John. *Reading with Speed and Confidence.* New York: Random House, Inc., 1972.

Watzlawick, P. *Ultra-Solutions: Or How to Fail Most Successfully.* New York: W.W. Norton & Company, 1988.

Wenger, W. *A Method for Personal Growth and Development.* Gaithersburg, MD: Project Renaissance, 1990.

Williams, L. V. *Teaching for the Two-Sided Mind: A Guide to Right Brain / Left Brain Education.* Englewood Cliffs, NJ: Prentice-Hall, 1983.

Wolinsky, S. *Trances People Live: Healing Approaches in Quantum Psychology.* Falls Village, CT: The Bramble Company, 1991.

Wurman, Richard Saul. *Information Anxiety.* New York: Doubleday, 1989.

Wycoff, J. *Mind Mapping.* New York: Berkley Books, 1991.

Young, Morris N., & Young, Chelsley V. *How to Read Faster and Remember More.* West Nyack: Parker Publishing Co., Inc., 1965

Index

fixed point of attention 3-8. *See also* tangerine technique
flow state 3-6, 3-8, 12-7, 12-8. *See also* relaxed alertness
frustration 12-2, 12-6, 12-7. *See also* learned helplessness

G

Gardner, Howard 12-9
genius 1-6, 1-7, 10-9, 13-1
goals 5-4
gremlins 12-2, 12-12
group activation 9-1
guilt 3-3, 6-7

H

habit 3-3, 10-1, 10-6

I

ideal attitude 12-2
ideal state 3-4, 3-6, 5-10. *See also* flow state
incubation 6-3, 12-13
inner mind 12-10
intuition 6-7, 8-7, 12-12

J

James, William 4-4
Johnson, David W. 8-2
Johnson, Frank P. 8-2

K

Kline, Peter 1-4, 10-9

L

Lao Tsu 12-7
learned helplessness 12-6
left hemisphere 2-7
limitations 1-6
limiting beliefs 12-1
limits 2-4
Lozanov, Georgi 12-9, 13-2

M

Maslow, Abraham 12-8
martial arts 10-3
meaning 6-7

meditation 10-4
memory 4-3, 6-13, 10-7
mental summary 6-10
mind map 6-10, 6-11, 6-12, 11-6
giant mind map (for syntopic reading) 11-4
mind probing 6-4
multiple intelligences, theory of 12-10
Musashi, Miyamoto 5-6
motivation 4-5

N

negative attitudes 2-9. *See also* limitations
neural networks 6-13
neuro-linguistic programming (NLP) 10-4
NOPS 12-2

O

other-than-conscious mind 4-3, 5-3, 5-4, 5-6, 6-3, 6-4, 6-6, 6-7, 7-4, 8-7, 10-3, 10-7, 10-8, 12-3, 12-10, 13-2
overwhelmed 2-5

P

paradigm 2-4, 2-6, 6-7, 6-13, 12-3, 13-2
paradigm shift 2-7, 2-8
paradoxes 12-11
Paraliminal Tapes 5-3, 8-7, 10-5, 10-8
perfectionism 2-8
peripheral awareness 10-2
peripheral vision 2-11, 10-2
PhotoFocus 2-11, 5-4, 5-5, 6-6
blip page 5-7, 5-8
cocktail weenie effect 5-7
PhotoReading 1-1, 1-4, 1-5, 2-6, 2-11, 5-1, 6-8, 6-13
affirm 5-4
close 5-11
enter the accelerative learning state 5-2
in business 7-5, 9-1
mind map of 6-10
origins of 1-4
payoffs 1-5, 3-4, 13-4
prepare to 5-2
requirement for success 1-7, 12-12

About the Author

Paul R. Scheele, MA, co-founder of Learning Strategies Corporation, is the principal developer of the PhotoReading whole mind system.

His education has focused on adult learning, psychology, biology, neuro-linguistic programming, accelerative learning and educational kinesiology. He received his Bachelor of Science degree from the University of Minnesota and his Master of Arts degree from St. Thomas University.

Paul is the developer of Paraliminal and Personal Celebration tapes. These audio programs use advanced recording technology to access the whole brain and enhance personal performance. Paraliminal Tapes are available through many companies.

He is an insightful public speaker and consultant in the human resource development field.

Paul lives with his wife Libby and their three sons, Ben, John, and Scott, in a suburb of Minneapolis, Minnesota.

He may be reached by writing Learning Strategies Corporation, 900 East Wayzata Boulevard, Wayzata, Minnesota 55391-1836.

Paul lovingly dedicates his work to his family.
Their passion for reading and zest for life inspires and
motivates him every day.

How you can receive a free tape and more information

Throughout the book I talk about the Paraliminal Tapes. They will help you get results in your life and help in your development of PhotoReading skills.

I want to send you a sample Paraliminal Tape called *Personal Genius*. There is no charge for the tape, but you will have to cover shipping and handling charges of $5.00.

Personal Genius helps you access the accelerated learning state for PhotoReading. Additionally, it shows you how to use the dynamic power of imagination and other inner resources to improve your learning ability. It helps get you into the flow state so that you can write better, study more efficiently, prepare speeches and presentations more easily, and think more clearly.

All PhotoReaders should have this tape.

To Order Your Tape, mail this certificate—copies, faxes, and telephone orders will not be accepted—to Learning Strategies Corporation, 900 East Wayzata Boulevard, Wayzata, Minnesota 55391-1836 USA. We will rush your *Personal Genius*. Be sure to include payment for shipping and handling. We will include a brochure of other Paraliminals and a schedule of upcoming classes.

Name

Address

Address

City/State/Zip/Country

Day Telephone number.

Form of payment for the $5.00 shipping and handling charge:
[ ] check [ ] Visa [ ] MasterCard [ ] American Express [ ] Discover

Account Number / Expiration Date